SECRET HISTORY

STORIES ABOUT KNOXVILLE, TENNESSEE

II

BY JACK NEELY

SCRUFFY CITY
publishing
Knoxville, TN

Cover photograph by Ed Richardson
Cover and book design by Lisa Horstman
Chapter illustrations by Lisa Horstman
Publisher: Rand Pearson
Associate Publisher: Charlotte Klasson

Published ©1998 by Scruffy City Publishing,
P.O. Box 692, Knoxville, TN 37901
ISBN 0-9650426-1-8

Printed and bound by Classic Printing Company, Nashville, TN

CONTENTS

~

One afternoon last fall I found myself at a desk in Knoxville's Lawson McGhee Library with several books open in front of me. One was an intimate history of Columbia Medical School in New York. Another was a history of the old Southwestern Territory. A third was a pictorial survey of ancient Syrian archaeological sites. As it happened, each had something interesting to say about one story I was writing about Knoxville. I used information from all three books to fill out a single passage about one obscure subject, a circa 1795 real-estate scheme here called Palmyra, for a story that happens to be in this book. It occurred to me then, as it has many times before, that it's a peculiar and very lucky situation I've found here.

I don't know what to call that situation, mainly because I'm not sure what the difference between a reporter and a historian is. They're both generalists; as near as I can tell, history and journalism are both, roughly, the Study of Everything. And, of course, no historian or reporter can honestly delude himself into believing that he's gotten to the bottom of it.

If there is a difference between historians and reporters at all, it's that historians have much bigger file cabinets—and, maybe, the patience to retell stories they've known for a long time. I think of myself as a reporter.

History can seem like breaking news. Sometimes it seems to move so fast, I find myself running to keep up with it, sometimes sprinting between libraries just because I can't wait to find the answer to a provocative question. And then getting it down on paper as quickly as I can, before it gets old in my mind, almost as if I'm afraid someone else will beat me to it.

Many of the stories that appear as Secret History are new to me as I write them. More than half of the columns in this second book, in fact, are stories I'd never heard at the time we put together the first collection, *Knoxville's*

Secret History, in 1995. In that book, for example, I have a story about Union General Sanders, who died in the old Lamar House, the hotel building still standing as the front of the Bijou Theater on Gay Street in downtown Knoxville. When I wrote that story, I had never even heard that an even more famous Confederate general died in that same building, also of recent gunshot wounds. Unlike Sanders, though, he died there six years after the war was over. (It complicates the question of just whose ghost that is in the Bijou.)

And three years ago I had no idea that one of my journalistic heroes, war correspondent Ernie Pyle, had ever been to Knoxville—and wouldn't have believed that, over 60 years ago, Pyle interviewed a former *presidential slave* in a downtown cafe. One that's still open. One where I've been eating breakfast once a week for years. It will never seem the same.

Three years ago I would not have suspected that the essential French existentialist Jean-Paul Sartre had ever come within 500 miles of Knoxville, or that he stayed here for a couple of days and wrote a provocative essay about America for the French press while he was here. Or that Amelia Earhart had spent a night in a Gay Street hotel, the year before her disappearance, and gave an interview fatalistically acknowledging the dangers of flight. Or that my favorite modern poet, New Englander Wallace Stevens, had found odd inspiration in a long walk around World War I-era West Knoxville. Or that one of the most popular playwrights for the early-Victorian London musical stage came to Knoxville to write an expose of the Georgia militia's harsh treatment of the Cherokee.

Because I was startled to learn about them myself, I flattered myself to think a few of these stories might cause a stir, and have hopes that they may yet. Grace Moore, for example, is East Tennessee's best-known opera star; before her 1947 death in a plane crash, she was a romantic icon of stage and screen. I discovered that Grace Moore's early childhood may have been very different from the pastoral idyll in the clean hills of Cocke County that she described in her autobiography.

Nothing astonished me more than the suggestion that the Svengali behind the early segregationist violence that rocked Knox and Anderson Counties in the 1950s was the imprisoned American-Italian poet Ezra Pound. Discovering his name in that context shifted the foundations of local history as I thought I knew it.

After 40 years here, Knoxville somehow keeps unfolding for this hometown boy. If I am lucky, it's partly for having stumbled upon such a fascinating subject.

All cities surely have a Secret History of some sort, but Knoxville's may be more complicated than most. Founded purely as a federal administrative capital, Knoxville later became one of the South's most business-minded cities, and still later got a reputation as a university town, though the college had been there all along. (With TVA, of course, Knoxville became a federal administrative capital again.)

It has been a city of remarkably progressive thinking that, at its height, built one of the South's finest public-transit systems, spawned industrial inventions that changed the way Americans lived, made national contributions to impressionist art and middle-class architecture, hosted what has been described as the first futuristic exposition in history, and almost single-handedly founded a major national park. And, hardly a generation later, or maybe even before that former era was wholly over, Knoxville was also a dirty, ugly, sometimes corrupt city with a seemingly entrenched backwardness that visitors found easy to ridicule.

Its paradoxes are deeply ingrained in its character and history. During the Civil War, tiny Knoxville was home to slaves, masters, free blacks, slave traders, abolitionists, Confederates, Unionists, all living within a geographically tiny area, even next door to each other. It's a city that was known for its harsh temperance laws at the same time it was one of the nation's clearinghouses for illegal liquor. It's one of the East's larger centers of higher education, but located in the center of a large region known for its illiteracy. It's a city that once had an elaborate opera house and log cabins at the same time, within shouting distance of each other. It's a city where mountain men sold ginseng around the corner from industrial designers who were changing modernist architecture. It's a city where eastern Ivy Leaguers ran the college while Western-style gunslingers fought it out in the streets and saloons of town.

Knoxville was always black and white, rural and urban, blighted and beautiful, industrial and agricultural, rich and poor, educated and illiterate, east and west, north and south altogether, all at once, all right here. Like few other places, in Knoxville you can talk about the whole of American history from Constitutional Convention days to the Cyberspace Age, without leaving the city limits, mostly without leaving downtown.

We've had actual, literal earthquakes here—a couple of them are described in this book. But as it happens, Knoxville's located on several other sorts of faultlines in American history, cultural tectonic plates that are always moving and scraping, generating the heat of friction. Then you get stories. They fly out of these subterranean fissures, like sparks.

I just try to catch them without burning myself. I hope you like this second collection of stories, first published in Metro Pulse between 1993 and 1998. I'd like to thank Rand Pearson, late of Reno, now of Europe, co-founder of the newsweekly *Metro Pulse*, founder of Scruffy City Publishing, who even back in 1993 was unsuccessfully trying to convince me that a collection of this nature would be worth the trouble; Lisa Horstman, our art director, who laid out the book's design and drew the illustrations at the head of each chapter; Ian Blackburn, *Metro Pulse* systems manager, who made the electronic assembly of several-year-old columns possible; my old Whittle colleague Nancy Harless, who copyedited the book; our production director, Martha James, who helped get it ready for the printer; Ed Richardson, who took the photograph of the Talahi panther fountain we chose for the cover; and Charlotte Klasson, who's covering the business side of these books much more efficiently than I did when I attempted the same. I'd also like to thank Joe Sullivan, Coury Turczyn, and *Metro Pulse* itself, for their support and indulgence; Janet, Rebecca, and Sam for the same; and Lawson-McGhee Library and its annex, the McClung Collection, and the dozens living and dead who assisted in research for this book, several of whom are thanked individually on the bibliography page.

Finally, I have to confess I always feel a little funny about having my own name attached to Secret History. These stories don't belong to me. They very nearly write themselves. They're so much fun to research I'm bothered by the idea that I'm ruining the experience for someone else. Knoxville history may wear me out one of these days, but there's one thing you can count on about Knoxville, and maybe the only thing. We'll never, ever run out of stories.

—*Jack Neely*

CHAPTER ONE

ACTS OF GOD & OTHERS

The First Trumpet

On Monday, December 16, sometime just after two in the morning, sleepers across the South woke up in a panic.

There'd been an unusual "stillness of air," a condition many were convinced was related to what just happened. A few who'd been awake just before it happened reported a light flashing in the west. Many recalled recent eclipses and the ominous comet that had unexpectedly appeared a couple months ago.

Even if there weren't weird lights in the sky, even if the floor wasn't shaking stuff off the shelves, there was plenty to be anxious about. The United States appeared to be on its way to a second war with a dominant superpower, Great Britain. Indians were rumored to be taking sides with the Brits. There'd also been lights in the north, the Aurora Borealis, visible even this far south. And for days, the sun had been blood red.

In Knoxville they said it sounded like overloaded wagons on pavement. Windows shook as if in a gale; things fell off shelves. People ran outside and had a hard time standing up straight. Some watched bricks fall out of their chimneys. In some places the earth swelled and sank, just like a heavy sea. Some thought they were watching the end of the world.

That was 185 years ago this Monday morning, and it was the first of a series of earthquakes more powerful and more prolonged than any ever recorded in North America. Mr. Richter wasn't born yet, but seismologists estimate that what's now known as the New Madrid quake may have been an 8.4 or even an 8.8, far bigger than anything California's seen.

One Knoxville man was staying at Warm Springs, alongside the French Broad River. His description is unusually vivid: "The fulminating of the mountain was accompanied with flashes of fire seen issuing from their sides, each flash with a snap, or crack, like that which is heard on discharging an electric battery, but 1,000 times as loud." A stream of hot water shot out of the mountainside; this traveler somehow measured at 142 degrees Fahrenheit. A 30- to 40-foot tidal wave washed over the French Broad. This Knoxvillian believed the earthquake was caused by "electric fluid." Finally, there rose from the earth "a strong sulfurous stench."

That account appeared here with this apology: "We copy the accounts of the earthquake at Asheville, from the *Star*," wrote a skeptical Knoxville editor, "as it exhibits the talents of the author to deal on the marvelous." But equally incredible stories were arriving from across the South.

By one theory, the earthquake was caused by a North Carolina volcano. Some blamed a volcano out west. Some attributed it to an Indian curse, "a Shawnee Prophet, who has occasioned it to destroy all the whites."

While "utterly disclaiming being in any manner shackled by the influence of superstitions," wrote a Knoxville editor, astronomical phenomena, the troubles with the British, and this earthquake "combine to render the present era gloomy and portentous."

Oddly, that sulfurous smell was reported at dozens of locations throughout the South, from Virginia to New Orleans. To some, the implication was obvious. Before 1800, Southerners had never been particularly religious. Frontier Southerners often shocked Eastern preachers with their blasphemous irreverence.

But with this earthquake, as one aloof local journalist wrote, "the timid took to prayer, expecting every moment to hear the sound of the last trumpet."

We didn't hear right away about the Mississippi flowing backward, or about a sudden new lake in northwestern Tennessee. For two months there'd be two more big quakes and dozens of aftershocks, an average of one rumble every day for most of the winter. In Knoxville at 8:40 a.m. on January 23, 1812, "many people left their homes and unfinished breakfasts, and fled to the streets." Things fell off store shelves, but it wasn't as bad as the one in December—or another yet to come.

"Another and Another Earthquake," went an exasperated headline in a February issue of *Wilson's Knoxville Gazette*. The earthquakes had ceased by spring—just in time for the war.

But one editor remarked, "A wonderful change has taken place in the manners of the people…. I think what has been done may be termed a revival of religion." In the year following the earthquakes, Southern membership in the Methodist Church rose by 50 percent. Church membership increased across the South over the next couple of decades. Is the Bible Belt of today the Earthquake Belt of 1811-12? I'm not ready to make that argument—but it sure looks like it on a map.

—12/12/96

The Pestilence

After a wet spring, the summer of 1838 had turned dry—and hot, every day in the 90s. The river was down several inches. Unreplenished by rain, ponds stagnated.

On Wednesday, August 1, recent presidential candidate Senator Hugh Lawson White and Nashville Congressman John Bell spoke before a crowd of about 500 Knoxvillians assembled in a grove on Methodist Hill, overlooking the river on the east side of downtown. These two co-founders of what was rapidly becoming Tennessee's influential Whig Party didn't disappoint their audience.

Going on 65, Senator White referred to his robust health more than once during a 90-minute speech condemning his former ally Andrew Jackson and Old Hickory's successors, the "Van Burenistas." Once the president pro tempore of the U.S. Senate, White had run for president himself against Jackson puppet Martin Van Buren, not two years earlier. Though he was popular in Washington, White's emaciated shape earned him the nickname "the Skeleton."

According to the editor of the *Knoxville Register*, White's speech that hot day in Knoxville "surpassed any former effort of his." But the younger

Bell outdid White in duration, delivering a two-hour talk.

As they listened, the audience on that hot day must have noticed the odor from down the hill, along the creek that ran between there and downtown Knoxville. There, 14 mill dams stopped what little water remained, putrefied with decaying grain and animal waste.

They may have winced at it that afternoon as they toasted the Declaration of Independence, Henry Clay, East Tennessee College ("the proudest pinnacle of the valley; long may the light of its aspiring genius glitter upon the mountains"), and the late George Washington (in silence, hats off).

They might have offered a moment of silence for themselves. Before the leaves began to change that fall, several in this august company, including the master of ceremonies, would die.

Among the first to suffer was District Attorney General Reuben Rodgers, 40 years old. About a week after the banquet, he was stricken with the "prevailing fever." He died in eight days.

The *Register*'s obituary column grew longer with each weekly issue. By mid-August, the editor observed that the obituaries tell "a melancholy tale.... We have been afflicted far beyond an ordinary degree with the ravages of disease...reports abroad have greatly exaggerated the sickness of our city. It is bad enough to be sure, but in our opinion our...friends may visit us with perfect safety." He may have known then how wrong he was.

For two months, they died by the dozens: babies, teenage girls, middle-aged physicians, elderly Revolutionary War veterans. There were no class distinctions: members of wealthy and famous families—the Whites, the Croziers, the McClungs—seemed almost to die at a greater rate than others, though maybe it was only they whose obituaries the editor of the *Knoxville Register* deigned to publish.

Then the disease crippled the *Register* itself. Weakened by fever, a typesetter dropped the printing stone on the floor, shattering it. One full issue came out with only two people manning the office. After that, the *Register* came out only as a "slip"—a narrow half-page, much of it consumed with obituaries.

The final death toll is unknown, but some clues indicate it was well over 100—a stunning blow for a town of fewer than 2,000.

Convinced that Knoxville was cursed by God, Mayor W. B. A. Ramsey published an anguished plea: "It has pleased the Great Disposer of Events to visit our beloved city with the pestilence," he pronounced, between his teeth, designating Friday, September 7, 1838, as a day of "Fasting, Humiliation, and Prayer." Ramsey begged that Knoxvillians "abstain from their ordinary pursuits...humble themselves before the Almighty, and ask that his anger may graciously be averted from us."

By the end of the month, Mayor Ramsey had lost several members of his household, including his nine-year-old stepdaughter. The whole city witnessed "unparalleled scenes of suffering" that reporters were too tactful to describe.

In late September came "a shower of rain and a fine white frost." Whether by divine forgiveness or a cold front, the pestilence relented. Many recovered, but remained weak. One was the great Judge White himself, so ill he couldn't soon return to the Senate in Washington. He eventually resigned and died a year and a half later, never having recovered his health.

Observing that First Creek was the epicenter of the plague, and that the stagnant ponds were "accumulating in filth and putrefaction...and sending forth the most poisonous exhalations from their surface," local scientists urged that the 14 mill dams in the downtown area "be demolished...at all hazards."

For years, the memory was one of those things people preferred not to recall. When Thomas Humes offered a narrative of Knoxville history for the 50th-anniversary banquet three years after the plague, he recalled "when the city reeled like a drunken man under the strong breath of pestilence" but suggested he be "pardoned" for omitting further detail.

—8/3/95

The Atmospheric Monster

There was no reason to doubt John Crozier's account of what happened that night. At 48, the former attorney general and U.S. Representative was one of Knoxville's intellectual gentry. In his house on the corner of Gay and Clinch was reputedly the biggest library in the region.

On Thursday, August 2, 1860, the former Congressman was sitting in a chair, leaning back against a locust tree on Gay Street in front of Captain Walley's cigar store, chatting with a friend about the upcoming presidential elections. Crozier, who'd been a prominent presidential campaigner for years, had been a Whig, an official elector for the Henry Clay ticket back in '44, but as the Whig party disintegrated, he jumped ship to the Democrats. Crozier's political enemy, Parson Brownlow, called him "this little scoundrel," believing Crozier was planning to assassinate him.

Brownlow lived just down Cumberland from Walley's, but Crozier didn't have to worry about encountering Brownlow tonight. The editor was an early-to-bed sort, sound asleep by 10:00.

This election of 1860 was turning out like none Crozier had ever seen. The Democrats had split into two parties, running Vice-President John Breckenridge and Stephen Douglas; the decrepit Whigs were going to give it one last try with John Bell of Tennessee, a familiar face in Knoxville for years. And the new Republican party was running a dark horse, Abraham Lincoln. The country hadn't seen a real four-man contest since '36, when Senator White—whose grave was just one block away from where Crozier and his friend were chatting—outpolled Daniel Webster to show at third behind Harrison and Van Buren.

It was past 10, but Crozier was in no hurry to get back to his house-full of kids. Walley's cigar store, on the east side of Gay between Cumberland and Church, was less than two blocks away; he was practically home already. Crozier and his friend were leaning in their chairs, looking south toward the river. He later recalled laconically, "There was a pause in our conversation."

His friend interrupted their speculations to say "Look there!" and pointed to the south, over the river. Crozier turned to his left and saw something.

"Suddenly a bright light illuminated everything around us," he later recalled, "as when the sun shines at noonday. A most brilliant and remarkable meteor made its appearance at the south end of Gay Street....As it approached us its color was scarlet, leaving a trail behind it apparently about 60 feet long, having all the colors of the rainbow...."

He said the meteor appeared to be "the size of a man's head and perfectly round."

Crozier continued his story: "Traversing Gay Street it appeared to be about even with the second story of the houses, and descending so rapidly I thought it would fall in the middle of the street immediately opposite to us. When it appeared opposite to us, its color became a cherry red and its appearance from being globular changed to pear shape. This change and shape struck me so forcibly I cried out, 'Look at its shape!'

"The meteor, as it receded from us, traveling from the southeast to northwest, appeared to ascend as rapidly as it appeared to descend when coming towards us. And to the eye it looked as if it was certain to strike the chimney of what was then the building of Mr. Henry Ault" (what's now the parking lot at Gay and Church). Convinced the meteor would hit them, pedestrians "were dodging in all directions, endeavoring to escape from a collision with the atmospheric monster. Those riding were equally certain they would be dashed from their horses, while those in buggies expected they would soon have to nurse the monster in their laps."

But Crozier was cool. "The reason, I suppose, it did not appear as if it would strike me, was on account of the well-defined line of Gay Street, it appearing to traverse above the immediate middle of the street—but I felt confident it would fall immediately opposite to me. I looked on at the grand display of the meteor without the slightest nervousness...."

On the contrary, Crozier claimed, "I was glad it was coming. Believing it was a meteoric stone and that it would fall in the middle of the street opposite to me, I intended to run to it as soon as it fell and claim it as my property. I was so selfish I did not intend that my friend...would share in the property but that I would make use of him as a witness that it was mine, and thus I would possess alone one of the greatest curiosities in the world."

Crozier seemed to admit the meteor's proximity may have been an optical illusion. "Under great excitement the mind acts very rapidly, and such was a portion of what passed through mine in a few seconds. To the eye it seemed reduced to a mathematical demonstration that, descending as rapidly as it appeared to...it must soon fall to the ground. If I had possessed a moment for grave reflection I would probably have come to a different conclusion, and some may laugh at my innocence and ignorance—to whom I can only say, if they had been where I was on that night, they would have been fooled in the same way."

Based on second-hand accounts, *Brownlow's Knoxville Whig* estimated the meteor had been much higher, 14 miles over Knoxville. Other accounts of meteor sightings that night have the fireball skating over the land in wavy sine curves. Crozier and others noted that about three minutes after the meteor's disappearance in the north came a rumble like an earthquake.

Judging by the sound of the explosion, *Brownlow's Knoxville Whig* speculated that it must have crashed about 65 miles north of town. They called for evidence of its impact, but none came. A century later, old-timers would tell stories about a meteor landing in Union County.

"Many people believe such things as meteors, comets, etc., foretell of wars and bloodshed," Crozier added, with a noncommittal caveat: Whether the Atmospheric Monster made its appearance on Gay Street "to warn us of the bloody war that ensued shortly afterwards," the esteemed statesman concluded, "I neither intend to assert, deny, or discuss."

—7/23/98

Acrobatics in the Time of Cholera

It had first shown up in Calcutta before 1820 and crept across Asia and Europe. It made its way across the Atlantic on a ship in the 1830s. In August 1873 it was killing hundreds across Tennessee.

One victim that month was a young woman named Smith who lived in an untidy shack on Clinch Avenue near Second Creek. She died only 10 hours after she began vomiting. Many were old enough to recall the cholera epidemic of '54, which had killed a dozen Knoxvillians a day. But this time we were losing only a few each week, maybe 30 since June. No one knew what caused cholera, but some speculated that since most of the victims lived in Knoxville's underside, down along the creeks, the problem was moral in nature: a matter of "imprudence." It was easy to blame on the bad habits of the victims, many of whom were poor people on the fringes of society, living down near the water.

Doctors were convinced cholera was caused by "the promiscuous and reckless use of vegetables and fruit": specifically, watermelons, cucumbers, and sweet corn, which were banned in Knoxville and for a mile beyond city limits. But there was a healthy black market Knoxville's small police force couldn't handle. Almost daily there came sightings of people flagrantly selling and eating melons right downtown, in plain view. Offered a black-market muskmelon by one desperate grocer, one man examined it carefully with opera glasses for what he called "sporads." He finally concluded he'd "take her, sporads or no sporads."

Doctors debated whether or not cholera was actually contagious. A few even doubted that the killer was cholera at all: One local doctor insisted it was what he called "toxicemia," or blood poisoning. Prominent physician Frank Ramsey, however, did believe it was cholera and said he had a sure cure: an ounce of sulfuric acid with about half as much of laudanum, the popular opium derivative.

Both Knoxville dailies ran columns on the editorial page headed *Cholera Notes*, citing the latest tolls from Chattanooga and Jonesborough. Refugees from more afflicted parts of the South arrived at the train station daily; Knoxvillians regarded them warily, looking for signs of disease. The *Chronicle* duly reported a description of one disembarking passenger, a man with a large boil on his nose.

The arrivals themselves were equally wary of Knoxville's liberties with food. At the Atkin House, across Depot Street from the train station, one refugee insisted waiters keep the corn and butterbeans far from his table.

Those trying to forget the threat, however, found handy diversions. In the lobby of the Lamar House, a crystal fountain on display featured "arched glass tubes through which alternate globules of air and water are forced." It was said to be stunningly beautiful and ingenious: "not one drop of water falls upon the carpet." A Mr. Magee was taking orders.

As usual, German immigrant Peter Kern and the Jewish-Hungarian Spiro brothers were competing to meet Knoxville's demand for cool refreshments, both offering fresh ice cream and cool drinks. And J.C. Duncan launched his handsome wooden racing boat from the wharf, prompting hopes that Knoxville would become a rowing capital. Duncan had named his boat after the fastest thing he could think of, the *Telegraph*. That might have seemed like a great escape from a cholera-anxious city, except that in 1873 the river still received a lot of raw sewage. People knew untreated sewage wasn't necessarily good for you, even if they didn't yet know it was the leading cause of cholera.

If you wanted to get away from the cholera, you could catch the next train for Wyoming. By one estimate, half of Knoxville's population had left town for the summer. Or you could just climb on top of a building.

On a Saturday evening in early August, some 4,000 Knoxvillians were crowded onto Gay Street, from the Lamar House two blocks over to Clinch, looking up. Across Gay Street, 40 feet up in the air, strong men stretched a single rope, from the roof of the three-story Ramsey Block building to the top of Dr. Hunter's Drug Store.

Just after 7:00, as the Mechanics Cornet Band played, the celebrated Professor D'Orville, standing on top of the Ramsey Block, stepped out over the crowd. He walked right out there, "with all the ease and nonchalance of a Blondin"—a reference to the Frenchman who'd tightroped across Niagara Falls.

There was no net, just a sea of upturned faces. After walking across, the professor went through a series of stunts: He walked across blindfolded. He walked across with a wheelbarrow. He stood on his head. He did something on stilts. "When he walked across with plucky young Woody Bowyer strapped to his back, neither flinching a muscle, the enthusiasm of the spectators was boundless." Money collectors hustled among the crowd, collecting silver dimes and quarters.

The professor imitated "a tipsy and weather-beaten female" and went tottering out as if ready to fall. But he/she carried a black bottle, and a placard labeled "Hunter's Stomach Bitters." Repeated swigs from the bottle appeared to give the character the strength and composure to go on. Dr. Hunter apparently sold a few bottles of the stuff that evening.

When the show was over, the crowd turned its attention to a group of "young Arabs," who'd climbed out onto a Gay Street awning to watch the performance and found themselves stuck there after someone closed and locked the windows behind them.

The joy of the big crowds on Gay Street surprised some, who took it as a good sign: "capital evidence that no cholera excitement exists here," the *Chronicle* editorialized.

The self-righteous may have felt obliged to revise their theories about the low-life moral sources of the disease two weeks later, when one of Knoxville's most respected men, T.A.R. Nelson, a former congressman and retired state supreme court justice, died suddenly. Judge Nelson would be among the last victims of what may have been America's last cholera epidemic.

—8/6/98

A Guitar, a Bone, a Tambourine

Even in 1883 some were well aware there was something a little peculiar about Knoxville.

From Kingston came apocalyptic reports of roosters barking like dogs, dogs crowing like roosters. But the editor of the *Knoxville Tribune* yawned. Such ordinary phenomena wouldn't even be news in Knoxville, he said. Just last night outside his window, he wrote, he saw a rooster "running down Gay Street with a tin can tied to his tail, yelping like a hound." Not only that, but another doglike Knoxville rooster "chased a pig down the street, bit his tail off, and swallowed it like he would have a worm."

He concluded with a statement we haven't found reason to doubt in these 113 years: "Many things that seem wonderful to the less enlightened are everyday occurrences in Knoxville."

Why, just today, in the putrid swamp called the Flag Pond, a boy claimed to have caught a monstrous fish weighing 369 pounds.

Of course, few believed things they didn't see with their own eyes. But then, sometimes that skepticism was the problem. Lee McClung was a black Gay Street barber who'd installed a modern plate-glass window in his shop. It was hardly in place before a "country fellow" unaccustomed to city ways walked right through it.

At the Mozart Sociable, a cornet-clarinet duo played the instrumental "What Are the Wild Waves Saying?"

There was plenty of reason to wonder. Toward Bristol, scientists from the Smithsonian excavated an unusual mound, discovering the bones of "a gigantic Indian," encircled by 11 other skeletons, together with long, buckhorn-handled needles of copper—astonishing anthropologists, who knew of no high-quality copper in the region.

Meanwhile, a "distinguished astronomer" was in Knoxville with an unusually large telescope from the National Observatory, describing the Man in the Moon. The astronomer "knows him to be a man," went the report, "as he can see him walking about." The scientist would happily show you his startling discovery, at a quarter a minute.

On West Clinch, gangs of men crowded the bridge over Second Creek, "making the night hideous with their whooping and swearing," blocking the sidewalks, forcing pedestrians to walk into the road with the horses and carriages. Sometimes they stoned pedestrians and killed domestic cats.

All that, of course, was commonplace stuff: Life in Knoxville, 1883. But up at 36 Market Square, bordering old Asylum Avenue, was tinworker Joseph Fraser's capacious apartment, and something different. At Fraser's flat that Monday night was an unusual visitor, one A.F. Ackerly, Spiritualist.

In Fraser's apartment, Ackerly made strange arrangements. Across one corner he draped a curtain. On a table he placed a collection of objects: a guitar, a tambourine, several bones.

Word of his seance spread around town. About 30 people, mostly professional men, appeared at Fraser's that night; they each paid a silver half-dollar to see for themselves.

Ackerly placed three chairs in front, facing the small audience. He invited two volunteers to sit—a woman sat in the middle, a man on her right, as Mr. Ackerly himself sat at her left. A second curtain concealed their bodies, exposing only their heads.

To one side a woman played an unremembered tune on a Victorian organ "to enable the spirits to act."

It didn't take long. "Soon after the music commenced, something began to rap on the table." The tambourine jingled.

Mr. Ackerly halted the proceedings, replacing the lady and gentleman with a fresh duo. This time, according to our witness, "the spirit began to scratch across the strings of the guitar, knock the bones, and 'do about' generally, taking the tambourine up on a cane and twirling it around in view of the crowd," then "throwing it down, overturning the table."

At this point one anxious man peeked behind the curtain—and, Mr. Ackerly said, "broke the conditions" of the seance. "The spirits had been so disturbed by this interference that they could not be induced to act again....They rapped goodnight, and the crowd dispersed." Out in the Square, witnesses disagreed about what they'd seen. Some were convinced it was a hoax. Some "were fully confident that they had been in the presence of spirits." And some admitted "they could not understand the proceedings."

"We are sorry that 'the conditions were disturbed,'" wrote our correspondent, "for we wanted to see a fair test of the matter."

Don't be skeptical. History is a seance, an audience with the dead we can only pretend to understand.   —10/24/96

The Beast of Middlebrook Pike

A century ago Middlebrook was a quiet country lane just beyond the western city limits, thick woods partly cleared as farmland. Just before automobiles, Middlebrook had become a favorite stretch for bicycle races, which sometimes drew hundreds of contestants.

In the summer of 1894, however, the beef farmers of Middlebrook were dealing with a peculiar sort of theft. Heads of slaughtered cows were vanishing from Middlebrook slaughtering pens. The rumor spread that a panther was prowling West Knoxville.

It was a troublesome spell all around. A rebellious Knoxville teenager ran away with a roaming band of gypsies, only to turn up murdered in Boyd's Creek. There was a rash of barn-burnings in North Knoxville. And downtown one afternoon, the men lounging outside Schubert's Saloon were startled to see Gay Street begin to move in a low wave, the asphalt near the Cumberland intersection bowing "as if a giant mole was forcing his way right under the pavement." It turned out to be a broken water main.

And people kept an eye out for that panther. On certain evenings, hunters peering through the dense woods just about a mile past the last streetcar stop saw something peculiar. There on the left of the road, just this side of Major Webb's house, apppeared a pale figure in the dense woods. Most described it as a large, white animal, twice as big as any dog—at least eight feet long, some said—and with a very different sort of head.

Seasoned hunters ran for their lives. One man claimed it chased him a full mile before he got home and shut the door behind him. It appeared and disappeared so suddenly, most reasoned it couldn't be anything but a ghost.

"That there is *something*," went the *Knoxville Tribune*'s noncommittal assessment, "there is no mistake."

A neighbor by the name of Day offered an extravagant reward—a horse and buggy—to anyone who might capture the ghost. Knoxville's curious, mostly boys and young men, appeared on Middlebrook, armed with pistols and shotguns, in search of the spectre. Spotting it, Sam Mays fired directly at the beast, but it didn't flinch. Everyone who saw the ghost ran from it—everyone, that is, until one Saturday night when two teenagers, Polk Blanton and Dave Menton, came to these woods, loaded for ghost.

They picked a post in a dense spot of the woods, sat on a log, and waited. They'd been there maybe 15 minutes when they heard something heavy just behind them, "like a wagon," they said, rolling over rocks. "Presently the ghost appeared," went an account of their adventure in the *Tribune*. It came within a few feet of where the boys sat before it "lay down and began to stretch itself."

One of the boys coolly took some matches from his pocket and lit a candle. It apparently startled the spectre, who "started off in a trot down a dark hollow." When they caught sight of it again, it appeared to vanish into a sinkhole.

The boys returned to report that the so-called ghost was "nothing more than a white bear." But that was hardly any less remarkable than a ghost. After all, lots of people in Tennessee had seen ghosts. Few had seen white bears.

Hardly anyone was convinced by the boys' assessment. After the *Tribune*'s account, readers protested that it was "a sure-enough ghost." Some neighbors claimed the Middlebrook ghost had been visiting them since the Civil War. One old-timer, a Mr. Dawson, claimed, "That haunt has been there nigh on 30 years." He said it had changed its color over the years: first it was black, later dark gray. Now it was snow white. There was even a legend attached to it. A century or more ago, Dawson said, a wealthy settler had lived here. Threatened by hostile Indians, the settler put all his money in a bag and took off running through these woods, the Indians on his heels. He ditched his money in the hole of a rotten stump. Every night, Dawson said, the ghost retires to the same hole before dawn. Find where the ghost lives, and you'll find the settler's fortune.

Middlebrook Pike became a popular place. Every night for weeks, 50 to 200 ghost hunters—some looking for the ghost's treasure, some for Mr. Day's reward, some for both—combed the woods, firing at anything that moved. A couple of cows were casualties. Even Melville Thompson, mayor of Knoxville, was there the night after he heard the teenagers' story, armed and "heeled to kill or be killed." But Mayor Thompson "saw a ghost *not*," reported the *Tribune*. "Crestfallen and sick of heart, he returned to the city…."

There was talk of invoking the great Captain Henry Gibson, the poet-lawyer then running a successful campaign for U.S. Congress; Union veteran Gibson was already held to have near-supernatural powers (according to one suspicious news story, the Emperor of China was seeking Gibson's military advice in defeating the Japanese). Concerning the Middlebrook problem, one editor opined, "By Captain Gibson's sword, the ghost might be run through and through and brought triumphantly into the city."

But both Dawson and his neighbor J.R. Powell claimed they'd "rather have ghosts than all these *people*." Weary of the trampled corn, slain cattle, broken fences, and all-night gunfire, the landowners began threatening to charge erstwhile ghost hunters with trespassing.

About two weeks later, the *Tribune* headlined a sad epilogue: "THE GHOST HAS GONE. All at Once Talk of the Spectre Stopped." The good people of Middlebrook got rid of the tourists. And if they got their ghost back, this time they were quiet about it.

In England, a well-known doctor contemplated a mystery about the ghostly appearances of a "beast shaped like a hound, yet larger than any hound that ever mortal eye has rested upon." But Arthur Conan Doyle's *Hound of the Baskervilles* wouldn't be published until seven years after the last appearance of the Beast of Middlebrook Pike.

—10/30/97

The Fire of '97

When you get a chance, have a good look at the 400 block of Gay Street, east side. It's an interesting row: a cluster of tall commercial buildings of different styles, some of them elaborately Victorian in style, some of them mid-20th-century utilitarian, some of them masked with urban-renewal-era blank facing. Some are gentrified, some merely preserved, some apparently vacant, and some, a big chunk of them where the Riviera Theater used to be, just gone.

Today the often-busy brewpub called the Great Southern dominates this block, which was advertised in the '60s as the *Promenade*, the backdoor pseudo-suburban adapation once mocked in the national press. J.D. Lee's gentrified law offices are also there, with his bronze Remington cowboy sculpture on display in the window. Kimball's venerable jewelry store is here, where it's been for decades. Between a couple of buildings is an intriguing alley—a narrow one with a metal facade that looks like it might be a good site for an eccentric antiquarian shop. In front of Kimball's is a standing sidewalk clock that looks Victorian but still keeps good time.

It's a place that looks like it has a lot of history. But as you walk the sidewalk from Arby's to the renovated Century Building, you can be reasonably certain that none of these buildings is fully a century old.

Urban designers recognize this central block of Gay Street as vital to any coherent downtown redevelopment theory, but in the last couple of months, two ambitious 400 block revitalization plans—the Clayton headquarters proposal and the State Street baseball stadium theory—have fizzled. Some say the place seems cursed.

City planners have long seen the 400 block of Gay Street as an especially sticky problem. But one century ago this Tuesday, the 400 block of Gay Street was a much stickier problem for Knoxville, because the whole block was on fire.

It had been a slow news week in April of '97, mostly out-of-town stuff in the papers, rumblings about war with Spain, news of "cyclones" in the Oklahoma Territory, announcements about the delayed state Centennial in Nashville. One big item was about the Chattanooga fire the week before, among the worst in that city's history.

Knoxville, developing a habit of calling itself "Marble City," was proud of the fact that it had never had a big fire. We didn't even have much of a fire department. The last time they'd had a serious job was a few weeks ago: they had used firehoses to quell the streetcar riot on Depot Street.

At UT's baseball field that Wednesday, the Tennessee boys lost to Zanesville again. The players made an unusual number of errors, some observed, because it was ladies' day and they were trying to show off for the stands full of co-eds. At Staub's Opera House on Gay, a wacky theatrical troupe called the Funny Chromos had performed a farce called "A Foxy Pair," as one impressionist did irreverent imitations of famous actors. Over at the YMCA, a reformer from the American Purity Alliance lectured young men on the subject of "Social Purity," advising them to be as chaste as women are. A minister voiced his outrage at well-founded rumors that Knoxville's police chief was in favor of licensing prostitutes. On North Gay, a big tent was set up for Professor Gentry's famous Dog and Pony Show, scheduled to open tomorrow.

By 3:30 in the morning, everybody was at home in bed. More than 50 out-of-towners were asleep at a new hotel on Gay Street called the Hotel Knox.

John "Chip" Davis was cleaning up in the office. The black man was a veteran porter who'd worked in several of Gay Street's already countless series of hotels. Working for the Knox in 1897 probably wasn't the high point of his career. Opened just one year earlier in a converted three-story merchandise warehouse, the Hotel Knox was a joint "of the dollar-a-day type," showy but cheaply built.

Around 3:30, Davis thought he smelled smoke, and began looking around for the source.

Meanwhile, Special Officer Gowan was walking his beat. So far the most exciting event of his evening had been a horse that got loose inside its stable on State Street. He settled that problem and walked around the block checking to be sure doors were locked. Millard DeArmond had been knifed in a poolhall just a block or two away on Central a few days ago, and the assailant was still at large. You could never be too safe.

Gowan stopped in at the only open door on this stretch of Gay, the Hotel Knox, where he found Chip Davis concerned about smoke. As they were talking in the office, they heard a crack above them. Then, in the back, Davis and Gowan found oil cans engulfed in flames. Davis ran up the stairs, toward the guest rooms, shouting "Fire! Fire!" He went from room to room, breaking down locked doors, but not as fast as the fire shot up the elevator shaft. On the third floor thick smoke and burning timbers forced him back.

Gowan called the fire department, only a block away, from the office phone. By the time the firemen arrived with pumps and hoses, about 4:20, the roof and the third floor were already shooting flames.

Most of the tenants got out. The office was confused with traveling salesmen in their underwear hastening to put on what clothes they'd snatched before they stepped out into the Victorian public. Several couldn't make it down the stairs. Some were saved with ladders from windows. Others jumped to injured safety. But for weeks, people told stories of seeing men, women, and children disappear in the third-floor smoke, just before the building collapsed.

The under-equipped fire department made a desperate predawn phone call to Chattanooga. Southern Railroad sent a special train, a flatcar loaded with fire engines and a coach loaded with firemen, to Knoxville. The train averaged 60 m.p.h., arriving in less than two hours, a record that stood a half-century later. The Chattanooga firemen were, incredibly, on the scene pumping water at the fire by 7:30 a.m.

Thousands jammed Gay Street to witness the spectacle. Fanned by gentle spring breezes, the fire marched north and south. The casualties were like a listing in a Chamber of Commerce brochure: S.B. Newman Printing, Cullen & Newman Queensware, S.H. George & Co., and Marble City Hat Co.; Sterchi Brothers Furniture, which was having a big sale on carpets, went up. When the fire entered the six-story Woodruff's Hardware—where the brewpub is today—concern about the dynamite stored inside was answered when it started exploding. Several spectators were injured by flying brick and glass.

The fire had already skipped north to the 300 block and was dropping "balls of fire...like snowflakes," which started small blazes on buildings across Gay. Concerned it might consume the whole city, men obtained a cannon from the Legion Armory and bombarded Arnold, Henegar & Doyle Shoes. Some credited the action with stopping the fire's southward march and saving Sanford, Chamberlain & Albers Drugs. But more than a block of Gay Street was a smoldering ruin of brittle walls. It looked a lot like Atlanta in '64.

Around noon, by the time the fire was under control, newsboys were already hawking the *Tribune* Extra to spectators, with details and sketches. They sold more than 2,000 of them that afternoon. It was already becoming famous as the Million Dollar Fire.

However, within hours the cost of the blaze was known specifically to have been considerably more than $1 million. A century later, the human cost remains unknown. The newspaper reported three known dead, then four, then six. S.E. Williams, a tourist from Springfield, Mass., was reportedly "burned alive." A. E. Weeks, a businessman from Rochester, NY; G.W. Roberts, from Pulaski; Major F.S. Harris, of Nashville.

Everybody at the Hotel Knox was from out of town, and the hotel register was ashes. The fire was so intense, according to one report, that it was "quite possible that every evidence of human beings in the structure might be wiped out."

Searchers did find some fragments of bone and burnt flesh in the rubble. They displayed them to the press, which published careful sketches of each fragment. Then the pieces went into a coffin, to be buried at Old Gray.

At Staub's, the very evening of the fire, A.C. Lawrence, the popular baritone with the Funny Chromos, inserted a last-minute addition to the program, a ballad called "The Fatal Fire." *The fire alarm was sounded*, he sang, *The steeds to duty bounded / The Hotel Knox was in a mass of flame…* Later came the chorus: *All honor's due / The Knoxville crew / The heroes of the day*.

Oddly enough, the troupe had been in Chattanooga during its big fire the week before. Mr. Lawrence had stepped forth with a song about that one, too.

—4/3/97

The Saga of the *Annabell King*

A few months ago, looking for statistical details about a shipwreck in the Pacific, I was idly thumbing through a book called the *Encyclopedia of American Shipwrecks*, published by the Mariners' Press, in Boston. As I thumbed curiously through an inventory of freshwater shipwrecks, one entry bounced out at me as only a line containing the name of my hometown can. **Name:** *Annabell King*. **Tons:** *86*, the entry went. **Built:** *1903*. **Date:** *Dec. 31, 1911*. **Cause:** *Collided*. **Place and Comment**: *With pier, Knoxville, Tennessee.*

I'd heard of the *Annabell King*. There's a fairly well-known photograph of her, circa 1904, a cheerful two-decker stern-wheeler with a pilot house up on top, loaded with crowds of happy passengers on an excursion cruise. The Gay Street Bridge is recognizable in the background.

According to one source, the *Annabell King* was in fact the 1890s favorite, the *Jane Austin*, rebuilt. But I'd never heard she was a shipwreck.

It was the wee hours of New Year's Eve, 1911. The *Annabell King's* captain and crew, whose names may be lost to history, got up very early that Sunday morning. The Knoxville Packet Company had just bought the well-known excursion boat to use as a freighter for downriver cargos;

this voyage, they had a big load of flour and salt and a half-ton of sugar, plus several wagons and other hardware merchandise, bound for Kingston and ports south. The sky was clear, but there was fog on the river as they left the downtown wharf at 5 a.m. They wanted to get an early start, maybe to get the voyage over before the holiday, and shoved off without waiting for a full head of steam in the boiler. They were going downstream, anyway; they probably wouldn't even need full power.

The *Annabell King* churned downstream in the dark past UT, past Third Creek, past the old Armstrong houses on Kingston Pike. Despite the low visibility, everything seemed all right. But the captain may not have known Knoxville very well. Worse, he didn't have a searchlight to pierce the fog and see what was ahead. For years, downstream from UT there'd been a bridge that crossed the river from Kingston Pike, just before you got to Looney's Bend.

The captain didn't see it soon enough. Seeing something very large looming up ahead, he gave the order to steer clear of it. But the under-steamed engine couldn't furnish enough power to make the correction. The *Annabell King*'s hull struck the rocky foundation of the bridge's pier. A hole torn in her hull, the steamship began sinking immediately as she drifted downstream. A few hundred yards past the collision, the big steamboat came to rest in shallows broadside to the river, the second deck and pilot house still above the surface.

The crew got to shore without serious injury, but the bulk of their cargo—the flour, sugar, and salt—began to dissolve in the water, perhaps to arrive at their destinations by less useful ways. The steamboat's new owners carried no insurance. "The loss," went the laconic report, "was total."

The wreck would have been visible from Kingston Pike. As West Knoxville enjoyed the New Year's Eve "Watch" that night, and New Year's Day parties that Monday, the venerable *Annabell King* lay half-submerged, sideways, humiliated.

On Monday the steamboat *Catherine P. Le* (not a misprint; *Le* was her last name) appeared with a derrick and salvaged those wagons. But it wasn't terribly big news in Knoxville of very early 1912. Steamboats were already seen as things of the past. They'd been declining in importance for 20 years, as railroad barons underpriced them out of business. Now another form of commercial transportation, the gasoline motorcar, was on the horizon.

Even some of the riverboats serving the Knoxville wharves that winter, like the busy *Economist* (presumably a more efficient vessel) were now gasoline powered.

Still, a team of engineers began the awkward work of salvaging the *Annabell King*, attempting to tow it to a nearby island, maybe Looney Island, to patch the hull just enough to bail and limp her to the Knoxville shipyard. They apparently got her out of the channel enough to allow the impressive 99-ton steamboat *S.B. Chamberlain* and its dredging convoy to get through to Knoxville.

But salvaging the ship was turning out to be much slower work than anybody expected, and then the weather turned cold, as lumps of mushy ice swarmed around *Annabell* in the current. Soon even the *Catherine P. Le* was frozen in ice at Paint Rock, eight miles above Knoxville on the French Broad. By January 17 there was a thaw, and the steamboat *Jerry* got through to Kingston, carrying the salvaged hardware freight of the *Annabell King*.

On the 18th a newspaper headline reported the *Annabell King* was finally raised—but the editor who wrote the headline apparently wasn't interested enough to read the short article. The word from the engineers was that they *expected* her to be raised. She wasn't. Weeks later the *Annabell King* was still half-submerged in the cold current near Looney's Bend, still dispersing her cargo to the river.

Whether she was finally salvaged or abandoned and swept away, the *Annabell King* soon vanished, as did steamboating. Folks who still remember this part of the river in the early part of the century say they don't remember a wrecked riverboat near Looney's Bend.

—*12/24/96*

Nearer to Thee

This week Knoxville's own Cyberflix releases an astonishing CD-ROM game called *Titanic*. Even if you can't follow the complex international intrigue of the game's storyline, *Titanic*'s still an eerily realistic tour of the gigantic ship on its last night, every floor and stairway of it, accurate down to the wallpaper designs.

I remember the sinking of the *Titanic* with the vividness that you always remember horrors, the sharp relief that comes with the first news of tragedies like President Kennedy's assassination. From my perspective, they happened about the same time.

It was in my father's garage that I heard the news on the radio, about a half-century after it happened. Dad was listening to the country-music station, and a song: *Husbands and their wives / Little children lost their lives / It was sad when that great ship went down.*

That song doesn't shake me up anymore. I don't dwell on it all day as I did when I was five. As a sophisticated college boy, I even snickered at that song. What would Southern hillbillies know or care about the fate of the Astors and other leisure-class socialites aboard a luxury ocean liner sailing from George V's England?

It turns out that some East Tennesseans, even hillbillies, may have known and cared quite a lot. On a tip from the virtual scholars at Cyberflix, I learned that one of the 1,500 passengers who died that night was well remembered here, even among Knoxville's least glamorous.

Englishman Robert J. Bateman came to America as a young man, working at first as a stonemason. His wife was a proper Episcopalian—but Bateman somehow veered toward Baptist-style evangelism, and earned a reputation for preaching. First on the invitation of the Florence Crittenton home, this young preacher with the walrus mustache and the intense gleam in his eyes lectured Knoxville's elite in the 1880s. He also preached to street people from the back of a wagon. Local businessmen, like tough-nosed utility czar Colonel C.C. Howell and wealthy gunslinger Major E.C. Camp, found reasons of their own to persuade Bateman to stay. Around 1896, Howell granted Bateman a low spot on Cumberland near the First Creek bridge, a bottom-of-the-gulley place that had once been a powerhouse for Howell's electric company. Alongside the Central Avenue "Bowery," it was one of Tennessee's most dangerous neighborhoods. Here Bateman established a rescue mission for all denominations, democratically named the People's Tabernacle.

Those were Knoxville's wild years, when the city hosted scores of saloons, about half of them within blocks of this spot. Just around the corner was Mike Fogarty's Saloon, DeArmond's, the Arcade. Here prostitutes, gamblers, and thieves preyed on travelers just off the railroad and the riverboat. Bateman was the pastor at the People's Tabernacle when Kid Curry came through town and shot two Knoxville cops in a saloon hardly three blocks from his church.

Reverend Bateman was known for his egalitarian charity—he once left his own overcoat with a shivering vagrant—and his resonant speaking voice. They say that even when he whispered, you could hear his English accents from every corner of the chapel. At Christmastime he organized shoe drives for the poor. Out of gratitude the ladies of Knoxville presented Reverend Bateman with a quilt—made of their husbands' old ties, sewn together. (Much of the Bateman family now lives in North Carolina; they still have that quilt.)

Bateman chose to settle his wife and seven children on the safer west side of town, eventually on Yale, near the university. His kids were especially fond of Knoxville; one daughter married a local pharmacist, and stayed.

Bateman himself was here for about six years. Restless, he moved to Baltimore, then Jacksonville, founding new missions in each city. He returned to Knoxville for a short time around 1907.

In early 1912, the 50-ish Bateman embarked on a two-month fact-finding mission to explore Britain's social welfare programs, his first return to the country he'd left in his 20s. On his return trip, accompanied by his wife's sister, Bateman booked second-class passage on the famous, unsinkable *Titanic*.

His companion made it to a lifeboat that night. Bateman remained on the tilting deck. There he assumed a role he'd taken in other dangerous places. As the ship sank, his sister-in-law heard Reverend Bateman's distinctive voice carry across the waves: "Let us pray," he said. Then, she said, the band played "Nearer, My God, to Thee." According to family tradition, that hymn was Bateman's request.

Bateman's body was one of only about 300 recovered from the icy water, alongside those of millionaires John Jacob Astor and Isador Strauss.

In Knoxville the People's Tabernacle held a Sunday-night memorial service for Bateman, featuring testimonials and a male quartet singing his favorite hymns. There was talk of building a new chapel in his honor, but it apparently didn't happen.

Bateman's Tabernacle survived and grew, though, and was for decades a handy place to take your old coats to give to the poor. It survived the Depression and even urban renewal, reopening in the late '50s in a cinderblock building on Central, almost adjacent to its original site. But fewer and fewer souls were here to be saved in this once-crowded neighborhood, now relandscaped in asphalt and grass.

Today the large white utilitarian building stands on South Central at the foot of Cumberland. There's a tall cross on the front wall and a weathered wooden sign proclaiming the *People's Tabernacle* in Old English script, announcing times for Sunday School, Worship Service, Gospel Meeting. A large, spreading hackberry grows alongside the church, its roots buckling the pavement.

If you show up at the church on Sunday morning, you'll find an empty parking lot, a hollow echo when you knock on the door. Reverend Bateman's People's Tabernacle closed in 1992, when longtime pastor V.T. Flenniken retired after suffering a stroke. He was the last of only three pastors the church ever knew. Today he's one of the few Knoxvillians who know the name of the first.

—11/14/96

CHAPTER TWO

UNEXPECTED GUESTS

The Summer of the Conquistador

J.G.M. Ramsey was the closest thing we had in antebellum Knoxville to a Southern Aristocrat. With deep-set eyes and the scowl of a man who's not wholly comfortable with the world around him, he looked like a Presbyterian elder—as, in fact, he was. But he was also a planter, a postmaster, a railroad promoter, and a physician whose cures had won accolades as far away as Charleston.

Dr. Ramsey was a busy man, but is best remembered today as Tennessee's historian. *Ramsey's Annals* is still handy on regional-history reference shelves, still quoted more than a century after his death. And maybe thanks to the fact that he could talk about nearly anything, Ramsey was celebrated as Knoxville's most impressive host.

James Gettys McGready Ramsey had a mansion as big as his name. Upriver from Knoxville at Forks of the River, he lived in a place he called Mecklenburg, and for 40 years just before the War he entertained an array of authors, scientists, and statesmen there. The first riverboat to reach Knoxville paid an obligatory visit to Ramsey's wharf in 1828. He became known as the "Duke of Mecklenburg."

Built right into an Indian mound, Mecklenburg was likely a peculiar-looking house. At its nucleus was an old log cabin; Ramsey built the rest of the house around it. Inside, Ramsey had some conversation pieces few of his neighbors shared. Partly thanks to the historical society he'd founded, his house became known as an "antiquarian museum," a repository of "manuscripts, relics, curiosities" of Tennessee's past. Visitors were sometimes amazed by some especially unusual curiosities: Ramsey's collection of Spanish armor. And although we don't know what it looked like or where he got it, some historians have assumed he found it in East Tennessee.

When the Civil War came, Ramsey sided with slavery, secession, the South. When it was clear that Knoxville was about to fall to Burnside's Union army, the 66-year-old Ramsey fled his home for safe haven in North Carolina. Almost as soon as he did—in September 1863—his beloved Mecklenburg went up in flames. A Union private was disciplined for the arson, which apparently was not sanctioned by Burnside's command. Lost were Ramsey's 4,000-volume library, a new manuscript of his history of Tennessee—and his "curiosities."

No one knows what happened to most of it, but looters apparently got some of Ramsey's collection out before the fire. Years after the War, Ramsey was taken aback to find some of his personal books for sale in a Gay Street bookstore, but he didn't have the heart to claim them. All his famous relics—including the Spanish armor—were lost.

What happened to it is as mysterious as where it came from. Spanish armor could have been brought over the mountains by American merchants or Indian traders. But some of it may have been dropped here centuries before, by the Spaniards themselves.

Like many historians, the Duke of Mecklenburg himself had puzzled about the route of the conquistador Hernando de Soto, who marched through the South in 1540, charting, trading, killing. De Soto's men kept records about their trip through this huge, fertile region they called *La Florida*. The mysterious place names the conquistadors recorded bear little obvious resemblance to the names English explorers found two centuries later. These journals don't chart a precise course. Between the last Spanish and the first English explorers, Indian tribes migrated, split apart, reformed. Place names changed. But there are just enough similarities in the place names and the scrawls on the old Spanish maps that hardy bands of historical vagabonds have traced de Soto's route. At least one has traced it right through East Tennessee.

For decades after Ramsey's death, most historians would have dismissed the notion that any Spanish conquistador credited with discovering the Mississippi River would have made it quite this far inland. Hernando de Soto saw much of the deep South on his final, quixotic journey—but surely not these remote hollers over mountains that are tough even to drive a jeep through today.

A de Soto commission, formed in the '30s, determined that Hernando may have made a little loop through southeast Tennessee, near Chattanooga, but then curved back farther south. A generation later, one of de Soto's henchmen, one Juan Pardo, briefly crossed the mountains into what two centuries later would become East Tennessee, but he probably didn't tread on what would become Knox County.

But 16th-century Spanish maps show stylized, pastel-colored clusters of villages on maps of *La Florida*, even up in these northern reaches, the parts that look like maybe they're East Tennessee. Recently, using data never before available, author and de Soto authority Charles Hudson compared accounts and redrew the de Soto map across the South. Perhaps Hudson's biggest digression from previously mapped routes is in East Tennessee: Hudson stretches de Soto's arc much further north and west than previous historians had thought likely.

In his 1994 book *The Forgotten Centuries*, Hudson states matter-of-factly that in 1540, months before de Soto "discovered" the Mississippi, the conquistador and an expeditionary army of a few hundred trooped down the banks of the French Broad; that they camped for three weeks at an Indian village called Chiaha, on an island that's now under Douglas Lake; and that they continued right down along the north bank of the Tennessee River, passing across or very near Ramsey's future plantation—and then "bivouacked for the night in what is now southwestern Knoxville."

Imagine de Soto, the Spanish conquistador, spending a summer evening by the river in Knoxville a quarter of a millennium before it *was* Knoxville. Trying to sleep over the racket of frogs and crickets and cicadas. Sequoyah Hills, maybe? Lyons View? Somewhere along here, de Soto and his men just might have lost some cursed Spanish armor in a spot where a gentleman historian would find it 300 years later—only to lose it, violently.

—7/25/96

In the Territory of Knoxville

If we don't think of botanists as international secret agents, it's not Andre Michaux's fault. The influential French scientist had investigated the natural world from Persia to the American frontier; he was already a well-known botanist before he allied himself with an unstable Revolutionary adventurer.

Michaux made his final journey to Knoxville 200 years ago this weekend. Maybe two and a half years earlier, he had first entered what would become East Tennessee as an undercover agent for the notorious Citizen Genet, the reckless emissary from Revolutionary France who took it upon himself to prod gullible American frontiersmen into conquering the Louisiana Territory then held by colonial Spain, to make it a French-allied independent state. Genet enlisted the aid of Michaux, a loyal Revolutionary with a perfect botanical research alibi. Genet described Michaux as "circumspect and attached to the glories of his country."

Perhaps forewarned that Governor Blount had denounced the conspiracy (maybe because it interfered with his own rival plot to seize Louisiana for the British), Michaux apparently skipped Knoxville that first trip.

We don't know for sure whether he was still involved in international reconnaissance a year or two later, during the weeks he did spend here. (By the time he first spent time in Knoxville proper in 1795, his old pal Citizen Genet had already been deported for causing trouble.) Here in 1795 Michaux drew a botanical map: "Plants and Trees of the Territory of Knoxville," eventually published in France.

On his final trip, in March 1796, he came via the Nashville road. Comments in his journal support the idea that Tennesseans already regarded themselves a "state," with or without federal approval. "This country ... has just been erected into a State, governed by its own representatives under the new name of the State of Tennessee, from the name of a very large river," wrote Michaux—just 10 days after the Knoxville convention concluded, and more than three months before Congress and President Washington approved their Constitution.

On the way Michaux stayed a night with one Colonel Mansko—who was skeptical of the French Revolution. Don't be surprised that European politics concerned Tennessee frontiersmen. Even in these hills, some were fierce partisans of either the Bourbons or the Jacobins, even named their kids after them. The *Knoxville Gazette* was then publishing combat accounts of the French campaign in Italy—signed by the 26-year-old correspondent Napoleon Bonaparte.

Anyway, when Michaux's host criticized the bloodshed of the Reign of Terror, especially the execution of Louis XVI, Michaux wanted to leave. "Although I had not dined," Michaux wrote in his journal, "I would not accept his supper, believing that a Republican [Michaux, that is] should not be under obligations to a fanatical partisan of Royalty. I was greatly mortified that the night and the rain would compel me to remain in his House."

Farther on his way, Michaux was so excited about discovering a dye wood that he described it in a letter to William Blount, who'd once condemned Michaux's comrade Genet as a "Jacobin Incendiary." On March 8, Michaux's 12-day journey ended in Knoxville. He dined the following evening with Blount himself, without recorded incident.

Then, on March 10, Michaux "took my lodgings in the house of Captain Louné near the ... River."

Michaux spoke passable English but sometimes got things mixed up. Perhaps recalling his caravan across the Arabian deserts, Michaux knew a place just west of Knoxville as *Camel's Station*. You can figure that one out. (Michaux was familiar with camels, having crossed the deserts to Persia on an earlier botanical expedition.)

Anyway, we didn't have many Lounés living here in Knoxville. But we did have lots of Looneys. Michaux's "Captain Louné" was likely Captain Moses Looney, the Revolutionary War veteran who was settling on Looney's Bend, the future Sequoyah Hills, that same year. He's buried in the Looney graveyard that's still on Arrowhead Trail.

The next day, Michaux "herborized on the opposite bank bordered by steep rocks covered with Saxifrage, bulbous umbellifera (low-growing herbs) etc." somewhere in South Knoxville. He later described windflowers, bloodroot, and a rare twin-leafed herb already called *Jeffersonia*, after the 53-year-old former secretary of state. "The time this plant flowers in the neighborhood of Knoxville is about the 10th of March," Michaux wrote.

Leaving Knoxville after a week here, Michaux remarked on the price of supper (two shillings, three pence) and fodder (two pence). We had American dollars in 1796, but British currency still ruled in Knoxville taverns.

Michaux soon left America forever, surviving a shipwreck off the coast of Holland that summer. Still "herborizing," Michaux died of a tropical fever six years later. In Madagascar.

His son, Francois Andre Michaux, happened to be right here that fall of 1802, continuing his dad's work in this exotic valley.

—3/7/96

Bathing in the Holstein

When he showed up on horseback that day, nobody in Knoxville was figuring he'd ever be King of France. A dark, bearded guy in ordinary clothes and unpowdered hair, just 23 years old, Louis Philippe appeared on the road from the east with three other young men.

He didn't look like a king or a prince. Heck, France didn't even have kings and princes anymore; in this modern age, if you even looked like a nobleman in France, chances are you'd lose your head to the Guillotine. That was reason enough for many Frenchmen to make the Grand Tour of America. And it's why these four Frenchmen were here in Knoxville, two centuries ago this week: Louis Philippe, Duc d'Orleans, and his younger brothers, the Duc de Montpensier and the Comte de Beaujolais, along with their servant, Beaudoin. Though they'd once supported the French Revolution, these Bourbon descendants of Louis XIII were now considered political enemies of the radical Revolutionary regime in Paris.

Just last month they'd been in Washington to witness the inauguration of John Adams and then visited retiring President Washington at Mount Vernon. For these healthy young Frenchmen, Washington suggested an itinerary which included parts of America the elderly statesman himself would never see.

The Bourbons knew East Tennessee was an exotic land, but they weren't prepared for anything quite like this. In his diary Louis Philippe described East Tennessee insects as "oppressive" and seemed annoyed by the "tremendous roar of toads and frogs" in the evening. The humanoid creatures of Tennessee he found to be lazy and graceless. "The food at the inns," he wrote, "generally amounts to no more than fried fatback and cornbread....There is coffee everywhere, but bad, very weak." He liked Tennessee sugar, though: *black muscovado*, or unrefined maple syrup. The scarcity of chamberpots in Tennessee taverns frustrated the Bourbons—especially one tavernkeeper's suggestion that when they needed relief, they try the broken window.

Around April 28, the royal refugees arrived in Knoxville. "Still nasty, inhospitable country, sparsely settled," Louis Philippe wrote. "We reached Knoxville early." (If he noticed convicted burglar Robert Parker being hanged downtown on the day of his arrival, the Duke discreetly didn't mention it.)

The Bourbons' visit didn't make the *Knoxville Gazette*. After all, they weren't the first French noblemen we'd entertained in this new town. They weren't necessarily the most interesting foreign visitors here lately. Just a couple of weeks ago, at Carmichael's Tavern, there was a real orangutan: "the first ever seen in this part of America." Knoxvillians lined up and paid a shilling a head to look at the ape, billed as a "Man of the Woods."

Louis Philippe's brother the Duc de Montpensier, an accomplished watercolorist, carried a sketchpad, but we don't know whether he made any sketches here in town. Knoxville "would be quite picturesque," Louis Philippe admitted, "if not for the wearying regularity of streets and houses in American towns." Knoxville was already laid out in utilitarian square blocks parallel to the river—which was, in those days, considered part of the Holston, a name many misspelled. "The Holstein River, which flows below the town, is broad and beautiful," Louis Philippe wrote. "We bathed in it; the day was very hot."

He made it sound like a pleasant dip, but as local legend has it, le Duc plunged down the riverbank naked, fleeing his bedbug-infested mattress at Chisholm's Tavern.

"Five years ago there was not a single house here," Louis Philippe remarked on Knoxville's sudden history. "Now there are over a hundred. We are lodging in one of the oldest, but laziness has so pervaded the way of life that they have not yet plugged up the holes in the outer walls cut for scaffolding when they built the house. There are five of these openings in our room, and scarcely a whole pane in the windows."

The fussy nobleman's visit, however, may have been Knoxville's first cause to be proud of its restaurants: "Our horses are indifferently cared for," Louis Philippe complained—"but the common board (where we are obliged by local custom to take our meals) is not bad." From Louis Philippe, *not bad* is high praise.

"We left Knoxville toward two in the afternoon of April 29th," he continued. "First we took a ferry across the Holstein, and then we halted for the night in Mary'sville (named for Madame Blount)," he noted.

From there the Bourbons went to Tellico, where they visited Cherokees, who first mistook him for *squonannah*, or Spanish; apparently, he thought, because of his full beard and dark complexion. With them he ate fresh strawberries, listened to the music of reed flutes, and watched a hockey-like game they called *hannatsoke*.

His interpreter was a local Irishman named James Carey—who, at that moment, was a secret agent in Senator Blount's complicated international plot to help the British take over Spanish Louisiana. Carey's fumbling of an incriminating letter would soon sink the whole conspiracy.

Louis Philippe's diary doesn't mention the Blount Conspiracy, but it does describe the Cherokee in surprising detail. Louis Philippe wrote that the Cherokees weren't very strong, were in fact a little on the puny side; he blamed their diet and the unhealthy Tennessee heat. Responding to European romanticism of the Indians as a super-race, Louis Philippe observed that "the supposed superiority of the Indians is only by comparison to the Americans."

Observing the diminutive size of the Little Tennessee, Louis Philippe remarked that it would make more sense to call it something else, and rename Knoxville's broad stretch of the Holston the *Tennessee* River—as it indeed became, almost a century later.

The Bourbons then traveled via the rugged wilderness road to the west, observing that locals called this wilderness the *desert*. By May 9, 1797, Louis Philippe was visiting a fort settlement on the Cumberland. "Nashville is much smaller than Knoxville," he wrote, "but infinitely better situated."

Louis Philippe, Duc d'Orleans, made his way back to France. In 1830, when former East Tennessean Andrew Jackson was president of the United States, Louis Philippe became the celebrated Citizen King of

France. During his 18-year reign, Louis Philippe was fond of amusing court visitors with stories of Tennesseans and their peculiar ways.

—4/24/97

Rather Singular

At 44, John Howard Payne was a big star. Born in New York, Payne had spent most of his professional life as an actor and prolific playwright on the London stage, earning a wide reputation perhaps comparable to that of Andrew Lloyd Webber. Payne's sentimental musicals made him internationally popular, if not always with the critics.

In his 30s he fell in love with celebrity widow Mary Shelley, the young beauty enjoying the success of her first book, a peculiar novel called *Frankenstein*. That obsession had cooled by November 1835, when Payne made an urgent trip to Knoxville.

As it happened, Knoxville already had its own Gothic history. Frederick Heiskell, editor of the *Register*, had published Tennessee's first novel, a Byron-addled Gothic romance partly set in Greece. (The novelist had just fled Knoxville to escape a charge of attempted murder.) And we appreciated Mary Shelley hereabouts. Only recently our Professor Foster was performing his own Frankensteinesque experiments, attempting to revive hanged murderers with electrical charges.

It wasn't Knoxville's Gothicism that attracted Payne, but Mr. Heiskell's press. He had to tell a story that wouldn't wait.

Like many European Romantics, Payne was fascinated with the culture of the Native American. Maybe suffering what we'd now dismiss as a "midlife crisis," Payne left the limelight of Drury Lane to live among the native peoples of the Southeast. He attended the Creek harvest festival and the annual Cherokee tribal council—a legislature held in a forest, presided over by an elderly chief known as Going Snake. Payne stayed with the Cherokee chief John Ross.

On the night of Saturday, November 7, Payne was reading in Ross's log cabin on the Tennessee side of the Georgia line, when the dogs began to bark. Some 26 Georgia militiamen, armed with bayonets, burst into the room. One announced, "We have business with you, sir!" Without mentioning a charge, the soldiers arrested both Payne and Ross and took them on a long ride through the stormy woods. "The movements of our escort were exceedingly capricious," Payne related, "sometimes whooping and galloping and singing obscene songs…"

During a rest, one rude soldier's song shocked Payne more than any other. It was a song Payne himself had written years ago as a soprano solo for a London operetta, *Clari; or, the Maid of Milan*:

"Mid pleasures and palaces, though we may roam," the Georgia soldier bellowed, "be it ever so humble, there's no place like home!"

Payne asked the soldier about the song. The soldier asked Payne why he was interested.

"Merely because it's a song of my writing," the prisoner replied. "And the circumstances under which I now hear it strike me as rather singular."

Payne and Ross were thrown into a windowless cabin in the north Georgia woods. Chief Ross was released after nine days. The London playwright was held for four more. "The evenings were almost insupportable," Payne recalled. "A violin was tormented into shrieks and groans" while the bawdy soldiers sang and danced. His only amusement came from hearing several soldiers try to spell the word *axe* (none succeeded) and to guess what country New York was in ("England, ain't it?" one concluded). They celebrated the Sabbath with gunfire.

Demanding to know what he was charged with, Payne was first told he was jailed for being an abolitionist. Later he was told it was for insulting the Georgia Militia, later for conspiracy against whites. Upon his abrupt release, Payne rode alone through the woods all the way to Knoxville, "where I had ample proof that Tennessee disdains the baseness of which I have been a victim." On Saturday, November 28, Payne wrote a lengthy account of his imprisonment and presented it to the astonished Frederick Heiskell.

The publisher of the *Register* cleared an entire issue to run Payne's account in full. "Such outrages call for the indignation of the whole community," Heiskell editorialized. "Without the punishment they deserve …an American citizen has no rights."

Payne's story hit Gay Street on Wednesday, December 2, 1835, under the heading "Outrage of the Georgia Guard upon the Rights of Citizens…" The story made international headlines and was reprinted over the next weeks and months in several influential journals, including the *North American Quarterly*.

Payne's days in Knoxville that autumn belong to legend, not history. He declined a proposed formal dinner in his honor, but one old story has him enjoying a brief dalliance with a prominent Knoxville lady.

Payne's expose of the Georgia militia shocked many and is credited with curtailing the militia's brutal tactics that the Cherokee had known too well.

Still, in less than three years, the most brutal tactic of all—the federal government's forced exodus of the Cherokee—was under way. It would be remembered as the Trail of Tears.

—*11/16/95*

A Quick Retort

We don't know what Isabelle Boyd *seemed* like to the wrecked men she left in her wake. We know only what she looked like, in two-dimensional photos.

No one ever fell in love with her picture. Her crooked mouth hid big teeth. Her Adam's apple was mannishly prominent. Her nose was large and lumpy. She looked something like an awkward adolescent boy, the goofiest-looking kid on the basketball team. She reportedly had a "loud, coarse laugh."

And she had a criminal record. At 17 she'd shot a soldier to death, allegedly for rudeness.

But "Belle" Boyd had *something*, and she used it without mercy, hypnotizing a string of blue-uniformed rubes to become the Civil War's most notorious spy. Some historians question her contribution to Confederate strategy. Some have denied she even existed. But no one ever forgot her.

The Philadelphia *Inquirer* ascribed her weird charm to "a smart pertness, a quick retort, and utter abandonment of manner and bearing...."

She and her charm cut a swath through the War's hot spots in northern Virginia, not always effectively but always memorably. She'd been imprisoned and had a price on her unusual head. By Victorian standards she was a scandal: a teenage girl riding alone, hanging around with lonely men late at night.

After Fredericksburg, Stonewall Jackson, her friend and idol, apparently decided she'd broken enough hearts. He ordered her to sit out the dangerous months to come in the more securely held South: specifically, her cousin's house in Knoxville.

Despite prevailing Union sympathies and guerrilla warfare in the countryside—and the fact that most of Tennessee was already in Union hands—Knoxville proper might have seemed safe for Rebel celebrities in early 1863. A Confederate garrison here supplemented the mountains' natural defenses. Even Joe Johnston, one of the Confederacy's top generals, was here at the Lamar House on Gay Street, planning his defensive strategy against Grant's invasions of the Mississippi Valley.

The Confederate Boyds were among Knoxville's most prominent families. Belle's uncle Samuel had been mayor before the War. Belle arrived at the Boyds' home—old Governor Blount's "mansion" on Hill Avenue—on a mid-February Thursday. Her visit wasn't a secret for long. Friday night, Belle Boyd got one of the most rousing public receptions any spy ever had. In the mansion's front yard, a brass band heralded her hideout.

"The people congregated in vast numbers to get a glimpse of the 'Rebel spy,'" Belle recalled later. "The people in the streets took it into their heads to call for my appearance on the balcony. I rather dreaded the publicity that would attend a compliance with their wishes." (Blount Mansion today evokes the simple styles of Blount's federalist era. But the Boyd's home then sported some fancier Victorian embellishments, including a balcony.)

"They would not be satisfied without a look at me," Belle continued. "So I steadied my nerves and stepped forth from the window. Hereupon the shouts were redoubled."

Not convinced that she could work her charm on more than one man at a time, she declined a speech. "Like General Johnston, I can fight, but cannot speak," she said, and that was good enough for the crowd. Johnston himself was apparently among them, the old man likely enjoying one of the War's gentler spectacles. The brass band played "Dixie" and marched off.

"Pleasant indeed was my visit to Knoxville," Belle recalled in her often-questioned memoirs. "The city at this period was gay and animated beyond description. Party succeeded party, ball followed ball, concert came upon concert, and I took no thought of time." Even one of her female cousins remarked about how "homely" she was—but also that she was a hell of a dancer.

She stayed here for several weeks, chafing at the Boyds' family rules concerning single ladies living under their roof—as 350 miles to the northeast, her associates prepared for a bloody encounter at Chancellorsville. It was soon after leaving Knoxville for points farther south that Belle learned that her beloved Stonewall was dead, killed by what we'd now call friendly fire.

More spying and further imprisonment were still ahead of her, then an official junket to Europe. Even Frenchmen fell victim to her *je ne sais quoi*. They called her *La Belle Rebelle*.

Legend pursued her more effectively than any Union posse ever did. Some stories had her becoming a Wild West antiheroine, even Belle Starr herself. As unscrupulous actresses assumed her identity for lucrative tours, the real Belle restlessly went through a series of homes and husbands and became a professional actress herself, playing the Rebel Spy to packed vaudeville houses.

—2/15/96

Sanders' First Visit

In 1863 the state of Tennessee was in one embarrassing fix. As the summer solstice approached, Union forces controlled the pro-Confederate bulk of the state. But the Confederates still commanded pro-Union East Tennessee.

Then President Lincoln got it into his head that East Tennessee—where some of his family had lived—was the key to winning the war. If U.S. forces could seize East Tennessee, Lincoln was convinced, "the rebellion must dwindle and die." From Kentucky, the procrastinating Burnside sent his young colonel, the 29-year-old William Sanders, to prepare the way.

Contrary to later simplifications of the story, slavery still haunted these parts. That summer, a place on Knoxville's Bridge Avenue was advertising slave auctions. East Tennessee slaves had caught wind of Lincoln's Proclamation, which was emancipating their cousins in other parts of Tennessee.

Disinclined to wait, several took advantage of the unrest and escaped.

As the Knoxville *Daily Register* reported that General Lee was veering well into Pennsylvania, local secessionists had reason to hope. East Tennessee slaveholders were so confident in slavery's future, in fact, that they were offering $100, $200, even $500 rewards for each runaway. By contrast, the reward for Confederate deserters was only $30—the going rate for the return of a stolen horse.

The chief of the Confederate occupation forces in Knoxville was Simon Bolivar Buckner. That parents in antebellum Kentucky would name a kid after a mixed-race South American revolutionary may seem more ironic today than it did then; when Buckner was christened, the original Bolivar was young and vigorous, feared and hated by European colonialists. The Confederate general likely saw no reason not to be proud of his full name.

Buckner himself was out of town that June, skirmishing near Cumberland Gap with most of his army. The remaining Confederate defenders were a motley group, regiments from Virginia and Florida, and a group of local volunteers, some military men, some not. The Confederates weren't all even Southerners. One combatant was a Captain Wiggs, who until recently had been a member of the Indiana legislature until his differences with Lincoln sent him south.

Sanders' Federals sliced through rural East Tennessee, twisting rails and hacking telegraph cables along the way. Tales of Yankee depredations from Loudon to New Market caused some worry in the stores and saloons of Gay Street.

Go to what's now the Baker-Peters Jazz Club, on Kingston Pike. When you get a chance between sets, look at the door on the ground floor, east side. It's got two bullet holes in it. Those were Union bullets, fired at physician Harvey Baker by men under the command of Colonel Sanders. (Whether the killing of this well-armed Confederate partisan was murder or just war varies with the teller—but the fact that he was shot inside his own house would seem to argue the former.)

Anyway, as the fog lifted at dawn on the Saturday before the summer solstice, Knoxville Confederates were startled to see a couple thousand blue shirts on the north side, and some big guns. Sanders's men fired cannon into the city—basically, what's now the downtown area—but most of the shells didn't explode—they just landed, *whump*. The Federals' assault "startled their Lincolnite friends from their dens," in the words of the pro-Confederate *Register*, but few civilians were injured. One was grazed by a stray bullet. Seven soldiers were wounded in the Rebel batteries, five of them mortally. Among the dead was Captain Pleasant McClung, an old-family descendant of both James White and William Blount, his legs shot out from under him.

On three hills on the north side of downtown Knoxville, Confederate howitzer batteries opened on Sanders's assault, two big guns on each hill, one insulated from return fire by bales of cotton. Finally, knowing General Buckner would soon reinforce the city, Sanders laid off. Via a freed POW, Sanders sent a message into town. "I send you my compliments," he wrote. "But for the admirable manner with which you managed your artillery, I would have taken Knoxville today." He might have added, *I'll be back*.

As he turned his white horse to the north that midsummer weekend, the bright kid in Union blue would surely have been astonished to learn that his name would one day be permanently attached to a hospital empire called a Health System in this city far from his home.

"It was a great day," concluded the *Register* on June 23. "We breathe freer, and our citizens feel a confidence in themselves to which they were strangers before." But that year, before the weather cooled, Knoxville would be in Union hands.

With the roles reversed, Sanders would die a week before Thanksgiving—defending the city he'd shelled back in June.

—6/22/95

A Swank View

Contrary to popular assumptions, I have a life. Knoxville's an obsession of mine, but not my only one.

Take my favorite 20th-century American poet. I've been reading Wallace Stevens since I was a teenager, certain he had nothing to do with my hometown.

He was an East Coast boy, a poet but also the only insurance lawyer to whom the bohemians of Greenwich Village paid much attention. Ernest

Hemingway, 20 years his junior, once punched him out over some insult now obscure. Stevens wrote spare verse with almost mystically vivid imagery: "The Idea of Order at Key West," "Sunday Morning," "Thirteen Ways of Looking at a Blackbird." It's the sort of thing you like whether you can make any sense of it or not, poems of such intriguing incomprehensibility you can read them over and over again and fetch a fresh charge from them every time.

I couldn't get enough of it. I wrote my very last term paper at UT on Stevens, and it was so much fun the A made me feel like a swindler. When my sister got married a couple of years later, I gave her Stevens's collected verse and sat out most of the reception in the gift room, reading "The Man with the Blue Guitar" to whomever might show up and pretend to listen.

Stevens was always refreshing partly because he had nothing whatsoever to do with Knoxville. That's what I always thought.

Probably the first Stevens poem most of us ever read is the one required in high school, a short bit of almost-free verse called "The Anecdote of the Jar." You might know it: "I placed a jar in Tennessee, and round it was upon a hill...." (That'll have to do. Quoting any more of it will get us into copyright trouble.) It's just weird enough to convince teenagers that all poets are nuts. It came out in 1919, became a buzz around the salons of the Village, and remains a point of conflict among scholars. Was it about art? Or nature? Or civilization? And what side is he on? And what does Tennessee have to do with it?

I ran across the plausible answer just recently. Some folks who make their living speculating about such things believe the poem was partly inspired by a visit to Knoxville.

Wallace Stevens was 38 on the last weekend of April 1918, when he arrived in Knoxville—apparently to attend to some kind of insurance-lawyer business. What we know about Stevens's impressions of Knoxville in 1918 comes from a letter to his wife, Elsie, in Connecticut: "From Knoxville, to the southeast, one can see the Appalachian Mountains."

Downtown that weekend were plenty of nocturnal amusements, like the Aeroplane Girls, the Trix Sisters, and Libonati, the Ragtime Xylophonist, all sharing a bill at the Bijou. If Wallace Stevens indulged in any of that, he didn't admit it to his wife. He implies that he spent his time walking for miles around Knoxville in childlike reverie, from downtown out to Lyons View, maybe an hour and a half at a brisk pace.

"Out near the golf club, at the western end of the city, there is really a swank view," he wrote. "The Tennessee River makes a great bend through woods and cliffs and hills and on the horizon run the blue ridges of the mountains. I saw no end of irises in people's gardens. There were peonies, tulip trees, locust trees, and an unknown tree, very large and spreading, covered with purple blossoms. You remember, no doubt, the pungent, slightly acrid odor of locust blossoms."

In Wallace Stevens's description, Knoxville begins to sound something like Shangri-La.

"I found lots of motherly old hens guiding their broods of ber-bers through the grass, already deep. And, of course, I saw many boys and girls, both black and white, loafing in pleasant places.

"I feel quite sure that I rather like Knoxville," Stevens concluded. But then he added that "the place is unfortunate in not having a decent hotel." (He likely didn't know that the grandiose Imperial had recently burned to the ground. The Farragut, which would replace it, wasn't finished.) We don't know where Stevens stayed—the Atkin, the Stratford, the St. James, maybe. "People in hotels of this sort are an amusing study on Sundays. They cannot make themselves comfortable either upstairs or down. Consequently they loll about, looking unspeakably bored."

If Sunday was dull, it was because that was the day movie theaters and vaudeville houses stayed shut. The only public occasion that Sunday was a parade led by the Knoxville Negro Band, from East Knoxville down Gay Street to Staub's Opera House at 3 p.m., where a lengthy program of speakers and music saluted wartime black patriotism. William Yardley, an elderly black lawyer and Reconstruction-era politician, was a featured orator. An article in the *Journal* suggested that blacks were exempt from white Knoxville's no-Sunday-entertainment tradition—because many had to work every other day.

Wallace Stevens was probably strolling among the West Knoxville irises then. But he wasn't blind. "The town is now what Reading was twenty or more years ago," he continued (Reading, Pa., was his childhood home).

"There are a few rich people, but…the farmers in the market, which I shall walk through in the morning, are the most extraordinary collection of poor people, living off the land, to be found in the whole country."

He spent time in Nashville, Chattanooga, and Elizabethton, but Knoxville seems to be the only place in Tennessee he liked very much. "I have always been of two minds about Tennessee," he wrote in another letter. "Sometimes I like it and sometimes I loathe it….I know well that I love the far South, along the Gulf, but this midway South is an uncertainty."

It's partly that uncertainty that appeals to me about Stevens. Maybe it's what intrigues me about my hometown, too.

—4/25/96

A Moveable Biscuit: The day Papa came to town and sent a telegram and probably ate some lunch

He came into this town from the west, driving his Ford Roadster along Kingston Pike by himself. He was a strong young man with a broad face and a black mustache and his black hair was receding from his forehead. He did not mind his hairline receding because he had many guns and he was the most famous writer in the world. His fine book about bullfighting was called *Death in the Afternoon* and it was new in the bookstores. The writer was not happy because some of the reviews were very bad.

He came to this town in the valley where the peasants drink the white lightning under the bridges and the leaders make no plans but eat lunches at Regas and he went to the Western Union office. Here he sent a telegram to his editor who was called Maxwell Perkins and he signed it *ERNEST*. The telegram that he sent his agent from Knoxville is the only way that we know he was here 65 years ago this week, and we know it only because the great UT professor Allison Ensor found it in a footnote and told us about it.

The writer was here because he had spent Christmas in Arkansas at the home of the parents of his second wife and had spent the holiday firing 2,300 shotgun shells at many ducks in the sky. His son was ill and thought he would die because the boy had spent his life in France and he did not understand Fahrenheit thermometers, and the wife of the boy's father took the boy home to Key West. His father could not go home with them because he had business in New York and he drove there without women and on the way he came to Knoxville and he stopped his car.

We do not know what he thought about Knoxville. The big two-hearted Tennessee River flowed through the town without dams and at the street called Henley there was a fine new bridge across the river and into the trees of South Knoxville. There was not the thing called TVA anywhere.

Downtown on Central Avenue that winter there was still a sad billboard that said *SHAMROCK SALOON - JUNG'S BEER*, but it had been there for three decades and no one had drunk Jung's Beer inside the Shamrock Saloon in many years because the Shamrock Saloon was not there anymore. There were no saloons in Knoxville at all and no bars where the writer could drink unless he knew someone and he probably did not know anyone well.

We do not know whether the writer met the young man called Cas who sold the pork sausage at 25 cents a pound and the JFG coffee for 29 cents a pound at his eight cash stores and we do not know whether the writer met the fine young fiddler named Roy Acuff or George Dempster, the man who invented the great Dempster Dumpster. If he did meet them all four of them would have fought each other because they were strong men and all four of them liked to fight very much and they all four hit very hard with their fists. That is one thing the writer would have liked about Knoxville in 1933, that even the successful men who wore the ties were strong men who fought very hard and broke bones when they could.

We do not know whether he met other people who were in the town called Knoxville that day. We do not know whether he met Major Neyland, the leader of the great Vols or who would have won if they fought. We do not know if he met the young Presbyterian from Monteagle called Myles Horton who was in town saying capitalism would fall or if he hit him. We do not know if Papa and Myles and Cas and Roy and George and Major Neyland had baloney sandwiches at the Gold Sun Cafe and drank bootleg grappa and fought and talked about fine big trout and argued about the *generalissimo*. They probably did not.

All we know is that the writer sent a telegram from one of the five Western Union offices that were downtown near where all the cafes and poolrooms and theaters were.

At the Tennessee Theater the movie called *A Farewell to Arms* had just closed. It had Helen Hayes and the new actor Gary Cooper. Earlier that week a woman from Fountain City whose eyes were clouded with tears from watching the movie stood up and missed a step and fell and hurt her spine and she could no longer walk.

The writer did not like the movie at all because he wrote the book the movie was based on and the movie had a happy ending which was not in his book and he did not like happy endings because they were not honest and true. If that movie had been showing when he was here he would have punched the usher and the girl in the ticket booth and the man who showed the movies with the projector and he would have told them never to show the movie again.

If the writer stayed in Knoxville the evening he sent the telegram he might have gone to the fine new Alumni Gym, where the great UT Vols basketball team were playing an exhibition game with the great Celtics. It was a very exciting game and the Celtics beat the Vols by only two points. We do not know if Papa saw the game or if from the balcony he shouted *Ole!*

Soon after he left he published a sad story about a kind-hearted waiter without hope called "A Clean, Well-Lighted Place." It was set in Spain and was probably not about the place called Knoxville.

—*1/8/98*

Dangerous

Passenger airlines were just a couple of years old, but already 17 people had been killed in the crash of a "giant" American Airlines twin-engine Douglas luxury liner in Arkansas. To a nation that didn't yet trust aviation, it was a shock—in 1936, that death toll made it the worst airline disaster in U.S. history. But the crash was felt especially sharply here, because among those 17 dead was one Knoxville woman. Lois Gremillion had lived on Hillsboro Heights, up on the ridge overlooking Island Home. Her husband, Stanley, was American Airlines' Knoxville manager.

Meanwhile, seven weeks after Lincoln Ellsworth's plane disappeared in the South Pacific, the dashing Arctic explorer was still missing. That week, the majority who'd never been inside an airplane were saying, *I told you so.*

That Friday's papers brought more commentary about the mysterious Arkansas crash, but also some good news about another missing plane: ELLSWORTH FOUND SAFE ON BARREN ICE SHELF. And that mild Friday, a lone woman drove into Knoxville on the Asheville road. With short hair and a silk scarf knotted at the neck, she looked like a pilot, and was.

She checked into the tall, 350-room Andrew Johnson Hotel on Gay Street. Some thought she looked younger than 38. Slender, with short, uncombed hair, she seemed to provoke everybody to call her "boyish." She wore a light-brown suit, a shirt with a "flaring Byronic collar" over her orange scarf, eccentric flat shoes with "brilliant stitching" in the toes, and a button on her lapel that said "99"—in honor, she said, of a club of female pilots.

When they heard she was staying at the Andrew Johnson, reporters from both local papers arrived at her door.

She didn't want to talk to them at first, but finally softened. When one reporter called her *Mrs. Putnam*, she corrected him. "I use my own name, please." Putnam was the name of her publisher-husband. Her own name was Amelia Earhart.

She'd driven from Rock Hill, North Carolina, to be on hand for a scheduled lecture in Lexington. She could have flown, but drove through here, she said, because she'd never seen this part of the country.

She didn't seem mysterious that day. She spoke slowly in a Kansas drawl but moved energetically—practically sprinted around the sitting room in her hotel suite. She was famous as the first woman to fly across the Atlantic alone, but that was several years ago. She was still flying, but her distinctions seemed increasingly contrived. Most recently, she was the first to solo from Mexico City to Newark, a trip some had criticized as mercenary. Here Amelia Earhart told us she wasn't planning any more big adventures.

"I have no ideas in mind for future flights," she said—but then she added, "There are always speed and distance records to be broken."

Long before highways, the narrow mountainside roads through the Smokies often terrified newcomers. The reporter asked Earhart what she thought of the roads. "I think they're excellent," she said. "Haven't had a bit of trouble with them."

Most Americans then depended on passenger-train travel for long-distance jaunts. But in 1936 Earhart was convinced passenger trains were doomed. "I do believe that railroads will be relegated to the handling of heavy freight on long hauls," she said. "Buses, I think, will probably continue in use for very short trips."

Everyone wanted Earhart's opinion of the unexplained Arkansas crash earlier that week. Some wondered if this was the crash that would convince America to give up on the idea of practical aviation.

"That was an accident," Earhart said. "And we all must expect accidents, because life itself is dangerous.

"Things even up," she shrugged. "One day there was a crash. Today they find Lincoln Ellsworth, and Howard Hughes sets a new transcontinental record. It seems to me that accident was only a regrettable incident in the march of aviation."

Her supper arrived: hot soup, spinach, and buttermilk wheeled in on a steam table. Someone suggested she go ahead and eat. "Oh, that's all right," she said, flashing her trademark boyish grin. "Pilots have to learn to take it or leave it till later. Let it wait." She wanted to keep talking about flying.

"It's not a bad way to die, anyway," she added. "Who wants to live to be 80—and get hardening of the arteries?"

Upstairs at the Andrew Johnson were the studios of WNOX, where Roy Acuff's Crazy Tennesseans broadcast their own show. They and the rest of WNOX's country crew were soon to be evicted for general rowdiness. Across the street, *Broadway Gondolier*, with Joan Blondell and Dick Powell (*"He goes Latin in Manhattan and roaming with Joan"*), opened at the Bijou. Down near Jackson and Central, a snake-oil salesman was demonstrating to a crowd that a real gila monster wouldn't bite a man who'd just taken a swig of his product. "Only 50 cents a bottle, gentlemen," he proclaimed.

North of town in the John Sevier freightyards appeared a handicapped white boy of unknown origin who could pronounce only a few words. One of them was *four*, a word he said once when asked how old he was, though most were convinced he was at least 13. Those caring for him were mystified by a gesture he repeatedly made with his hands, two fingers rising into the air, then tumbling to the ground. They speculated that he'd witnessed an accident in the freightyards, someone falling from a trestle.

Meanwhile, Earhart checked out of the Andrew Johnson and drove to Lexington, soon to meet her husband in time for their fifth anniversary. She never had to worry about hardening of the arteries, of course. Whether she knew it or not, her husband, George Putnam, was already planning her round-the-equator flight for next year.

Eighteen months after she checked out of the Andrew Johnson, the world was looking for Amelia Earhart. Maybe she wouldn't have wanted to be here now, 60 summers later, at the age of 100. But we've never wholly given up on her.

—8/28/97

Ernie and Bill

Long before dawn that cold morning in early 1937, the old bald man we knew as Uncle Bill left his rented room near Knoxville College, as he did every morning, to come to Weaver's Grill on Union Avenue and bake pies.

Over lunch that day, some customers may have been reading about Ernie Pyle's adventures in Oklahoma in his syndicated column in the *News-Sentinel*, when a stranger entered and passed toward the back. The white man in the trench coat was here on business. His thinning hair already going gray; he looked older than 36.

Some may have looked up when he sat in the back room of the restaurant with a pad of paper and spent a long time chatting with Uncle Bill.

The man in the trench coat, the roving columnist known by name but not by face to his readers, was Ernie Pyle himself. Writing travel dispatches for newspapers nationwide, he always displayed a wry wit and a sympathy for regular folks.

He was from Indiana, but seemed especially interested in this part of the country. He'd been here about a year earlier, to write about the construction of Norris Dam. Yesterday he'd gone up to see his "old friend" again and remarked on how lonely and dull a dam looks when it's finished.

In five or six years, he would be America's best-known war correspondent, so close to the front lines he was almost always photographed wearing a helmet. But in 1937 there was no war. In Knoxville Ernie Pyle wore a fedora.

"Uncle Bill," the pastry chef Pyle found so interesting, was born William Andrew Johnson. He'd been a slave of President Andrew Johnson, named by Johnson himself, *for* himself, back before the Civil War. In 1937 William Andrew Johnson believed himself to be the last surviving slave of a U.S. president. (The fact that he'd been a slave of Abraham Lincoln's vice-president probably struck no one as ironic—certainly no one raised in East Tennessee.)

William had stayed with the Johnson family in Greeneville into the 1880s, years after abolition, and moved down to Knoxville. He was already close to 70 when he became a publicity gimmick for the new Andrew Johnson Hotel on Gay Street: the ex-slave of Andrew Johnson, hired as doorman for the Andrew Johnson Hotel. But William eventually got tired of standing up all day and gave it up to take a job baking—a skill he'd learned as a slave.

"When I was little, Mr. Andrew used to hold me on one knee and my sister on the other, and he'd rub our heads and laugh...." William Andrew Johnson told Pyle at Weaver's. "One day, Mrs. Johnson called us all in and said we were free now. She said we were free to go, or we could stay if we wanted to."

Pyle scribbled it all down and wrote it up for next Thursday's column. "William Andrew Johnson is a happy old man with a distinction," he wrote. "He is, so far as he knows, the only living ex-slave of a president..." Pyle's column appeared without comment in the *News-Sentinel* and dozens of other papers nationwide. "William came to Knoxville many years ago. He never married, and he has no relatives at all now....

"William had a keen disappointment last spring. President Roosevelt came to Knoxville to dedicate Norris Dam. William got it into his head that he wanted to shake hands with the President and tell him he was once a slave of a President. William thought President Roosevelt might be agreeable to shaking hands with him.

"So he went to some of his white friends—some big men in the Chamber of Commerce—and asked them if they would fix it up. They told William they would try, but they didn't think anything could be done. Later they reported back that such a thing was impossible. William was upset about it.

"Of course it wasn't impossible at all. William should have known better than to ask a Chamber of Commerce man. He should have asked a newspaper man."

The story about Pyle's lunch with Uncle Bill at Weaver's caught the eye of at least one influential reader: Franklin Roosevelt himself, who immediately sent Secret Service agents to Knoxville to pay Uncle Bill's way for an official White House visit. When the train arrived in Washington, reporters swarmed to get a picture of the pastry chef from Weaver's. But obliging Secret Service agents had given Uncle Bill a porter's outfit to allow him to slip through the mobs unrecognized.

Bill Johnson had an unexpectedly lengthy audience with President Roosevelt; he commented that Andrew Johnson's White House of the 1860s "wasn't nothing as compared to the White House doin's today."

Pyle didn't record William's words in phonetic dialect, but other reporters did—though they allowed that his accent was unlike "the typical Southern Negro dialect."

Roosevelt presented Johnson with a silver-headed cane inscribed with FDR's name. "Mr. Roosevelt's jist my kind of white folks," William was quoted as saying. "He 'minds me a heap of Marse Johnson. I'd hate to see him in sich trouble as Marse Johnson got into...."

Pyle told his readers that this was "the happiest I've ever inadvertently made anybody." William was a sudden celebrity, interviewed on nationwide radio. But his fame didn't last long. As the war started, William was in a home for the indigent, no longer able to walk or support himself with a job. Popular columnist Bert Vincent wrote a column pleading that someone donate a wheelchair to Uncle Bill.

William Andrew Johnson died in May 1943, thought to be 87. Ernie Pyle, the man who interviewed Uncle Bill at Weaver's, died less than two years later, shot by a Japanese sniper at Ie Shima.

But Weaver's Grill, the restaurant on Union Avenue, is still there, with a different name. It's now known as Pete's Coffee Shop, still crowded at lunchtime, even in that back room where Ernie Pyle met Bill Johnson, and it's still well known for its homemade lemon pies.

—1/30/97

JACK NEELY

The Knoxistentialist

Over the holidays, I found myself in somebody's kitchen trying to justify my peculiar career to a newcomer. "Knoxville history is the study of everything," I explained. I mentioned nuclear physics, American literature, slavery and abolition, country music, innovative banking practices.

"How about French existentialism?" she demanded. My heart skipped a beat. Knoxvillians and French existentialists would seem to have nothing in common except that they all drink a whole lot of coffee. She thought she had me there, but I'd had some punch and was in no mood to back down. "Heck," I said. "Even Jean-Paul Sartre was right here in Knoxville!" Concerned that she might actually believe me, I added, "He wrote about Knoxville for *Le Figaro!*"

I should have stopped there, but didn't. "Sure, that's right!" Full of Dutch courage and maybe a subconscious need to let her know I was bluffing, I added, "Sure, Jean-Paul Sartre was in Knoxville, and he landed at McGhee Tyson Airport in a B-29!" Weird as it is to think of Sartre in Knoxville, it's weirder to picture him climbing out of a World War II American bomber. I hoped the conversation would dissolve into sly existential absurdism, my usual escape hatch.

But she didn't let me off the hook. "Prove it!" she demanded.

I went to the library in a cold sweat. It took a couple of hours to work through, but like all wild hunches about Knoxville, it's all true.

Jean-Paul Sartre was 39 years old in early 1945, just becoming world famous as the author of the novel *Nausea* and the essay "Being and Nothingness," when he touched down here in a State Department-sponsored B-29 early on his first tour of America. Sartre didn't get around that much. This was, in fact, one leg of the first airplane trip of his life, with a press junket from liberated France to survey the American war effort. That winter he stopped in New York, then Baltimore—then Knoxville.

The short, wall-eyed Frenchman was one of dozens of international intellectuals who turned our heads on Market Street in those days: India's Jawaharlal Nehru, Israel's David Ben-Gurion, Swiss architect le Corbusier. Often-controversial author John Gunther was here just weeks after Sartre was. They all came to Knoxville for the same reason—and that was to see what Sartre habitually called "Roosevelt's TVA."

We sometimes forget that our utility company was once a global sensation. To Sartre and some others, the success of TVA was revolutionary, more interesting than the success of the Allied armies. Sartre's articles about TVA were published in a French magazine called *Combat*—not a comic book, but Albert Camus' own intellectual journal. I haven't been able to find a full copy. (Sartre is quoted as hailing TVA as a "democratic effort" and a "vast cooperative," but I'm not sure whether Sartre's full assessment of TVA is available in English.)

Some of the fruits of his American Odyssey, however, are handy in the public library. One essay called "American Cities," published in *Le Figaro* in 1945, mentions Knoxville and about a dozen other towns that made some sort of impression on him. Speaking of the origin of American cities as temporary outposts, Sartre writes, "Detroit and Minneapolis, Knoxville and Memphis were all *born temporary* and have stayed that way."

He wasn't very specific about Knoxville in that essay, but everything he says about "American cities" would be familiar to any Knoxvillian in 1945: "It is customary...for the fashionable neighborhoods to slide from the center to the outskirts of the city; after five years the center of town is 'polluted.' If you walk about there, you come upon tumble-down houses that retain a pretentious look beneath their filth; you find a complicated kind of architecture, one-story frame houses with entrances formed by peristyles supported by columns, gothic chalets, 'Colonial houses,' etc. These were formerly aristocratic homes, now inhabited by the poor."

In this essay, however, Sartre gave more attention to one "American City" than any other: Fontana, the instant community on the North Carolina side of the Smokies, built during the war. Sartre described Fontana to his wartime France as "an artificial town built about a great dam in Tennessee." (That error's understandable for a guy who knows no English, driven by locals to a spot just across the North Carolina border.) In his meditation on America's peculiar temporariness, the instant, ready-made village of Fontana became a symbol for the whole country. American homes, he said, "hastily constructed and made expressly to be hastily demolished, obviously bear a strange resemblance to Fontana." He takes that idea even further: "Detroit and Minneapolis are Fontanas which have had luck," he wrote. For decades Sartre would remark to Parisian friends about the strange scene that was Fontana.

Sartre predicted America's postwar suburban sprawl and described the disposable culture that Alvin Toffler described 25 years later in *Future Shock*. America was like Fontana, he said, without a heritage, without a culture. For Europeans like himself, he wrote, "a city is, above all, a past"—but not in America. If only our cities seemed more historic, Sartre wrote, Americans "could find a social past, a tradition...."

From Fontana, Sartre returned to Knoxville. (Unaccustomed to so much motorized travel, he said he felt like a parcel during his American trip.) I haven't learned where he stayed, whether at a private home or a hotel: the Andrew Johnson or the Farragut, maybe. But while he was in Knoxville, Sartre apparently wrote another essay, "Individualism and Conformism in the United States," in which he describes East Tennessee's war propaganda billboards as admirably subtler than the ones the Nazis had put up back home. (In the same essay, he characterizes idealistic Americans anticipating some future of world peace as naive dimwits. "I believe in the existence of evil and they do not," he wrote.)

The question remains of where Sartre hung out during his time here. I'd like to think Sartre found time for some JFG Gourmet Blend at a small table at the Farragut Cafe, discussing ontology with Homer and Jethro.

—1/16/97

The One-Eyed Woman

In the September/October issue of *American Photo*, there's a lengthy cover story about the great French photographer Henri Cartier-Bresson.

If you don't know his name, it's safe to say you know his work. Called the most influential photojournalist of the century, he photographed many of the political and intellectual giants of his day: DeGaulle, Picasso, Matisse, Gandhi. His work is often reprinted on book covers and in magazines, and his well-known principle of capturing *the Decisive Moment* is taught in college. What Cartier-Bresson could do with a hand-held Leica, when serious photographers always set shots up with tripods, astonished people.

The work in this particular *American Photo* feature concentrates mostly on his provocative street scenes: Paris, Berlin, Rome, Naples. There are a few American pictures, including one portrait of Marilyn Monroe in Reno.

But the largest and most striking image in the whole feature is another American scene, reprinted here across a two-page spread. Students of Cartier-Bresson's work say they've never seen it before. This big one is a black-and-white shot of an attractive woman in a fur coat and an elegant '40s hairdo in the driver's seat of a car, in an urban street of pawnshops and cheap jewelers. She's looking out her driver's door window, toward you. She doesn't look happy. But what startles you about the picture is that the woman's wearing an ugly white bandage taped over her left eye.

The picture is titled *Knoxville, Tennessee, 1946.*

Cartier-Bresson is still alive. This Friday he turns 89. I'd give him a call, but he lives in Paris and they say he doesn't give interviews. From other sources, we know a little about how he happened to be here.

When he was in Knoxville, Cartier-Bresson was 38 years old. He'd already worked with the great French director Jean Renoir; in 1940 he was captured by the Nazis but eventually escaped a prison camp to join the French *Resistance.* In 1946 his work was so well known that New York's Museum of Modern Art had mounted a Cartier-Bresson retrospective. A *posthumous* retrospective, in fact, the consequence of a rumor that Cartier-Bresson had been killed in the war.

It was, of course, more than half a century premature. Cartier-Bresson came stateside, partly to straighten out those doodahs at the MOMA. While he was in New York, Cartier-Bresson linked up with another journalist who persuaded the photographer to join him on a whirlwind road-trip around the U.S.A.

That he'd been in Tennessee is no surprise. Cartier-Bresson's arresting pictures of rural Tennessee appear in several books: a hillside junkyard full of pre-war sedans behind a white cross that says JESUS IS COMING SOON; a large black woman on a rustic porch.

From Tennessee Cartier-Bresson took a swing through Mississippi, a trip that produced a photo of a young, nubile Truman Capote, and what's probably the most famous photo of William Faulkner, the one you see on book covers with his skinny little dogs in the yard.

Why he came to Knoxville I can only guess. Jean-Paul Sartre, whom Cartier-Bresson had recently photographed, had been here the previous year, mainly to see TVA. Sartre mentioned Knoxville in some essays published in France. Maybe during that Paris shoot Sartre urged Cartier-Bresson, *vous absolutement muste visitez le Knoxville.* Or maybe the photographer was curious about Oak Ridge's Manhattan Project or Chet Atkins's picking style—or, for all I know, Coach Neyland's Orange Bowl-bound Tennessee Vols.

But what Cartier-Bresson found in Knoxville was a voguish lady with an eyepatch.

The more you look at her, the more unlikely she seems. This stylish woman seated in the driver's seat, with her right hand on the wheel, looking around as if to pull into traffic—but she's obviously not ready to do any driving at the moment, because there's a large crate of some kind on her hood. And even though she's glamorously dressed in fur and made up with plucked eyebrows and heart-shaped lipstick, her car isn't in very good shape, rusted out around the holes where the rear-view mirror used to be.

Nearby is Cole Drug Store and Southern Credit Jewelers. In 1946 both of those businesses were at the southwest corner of Market Square, where the Soup Kitchen is now. The lady's car was backed up alongside all the other farmers' trucks that used to park on both sides of the old Market House.

In the photograph Home Federal's sign is in the background; that bank's still in the same location today, though in a newer building. Deeper in the background, two blocks away at Market and Church, is the tall, brick Bank of Knoxville Building, today occupied by BankFirst.

Carry the magazine out into Market Square and it's easy to find the spot where Cartier-Bresson stood. Stand between the concrete-step fountain and the Union Avenue end of Watson's, look south, and it all shifts into focus.

If Cartier-Bresson returns to this spot this year, he'll find plenty of subjects. The fiery-eyed street preachers who materialize every day at 11:30; the lunch clusters of identically dressed bankers, all hands plunged in pockets; the happy old guy with the thick glasses and the *New York Times* bag who makes his rounds in the mornings; the Leaner, the homeless man with a prophet's beard who listens to buildings and talks to angels; the officious young police recruits ticketing cars on Market Street.

It's not much of a trip to that spot for us at *Metro Pulse*; prominent in the near background looms the Arnstein Building, where we write this stuff up. If I'd worked for TVA in 1946, I could have looked out this same window and seen Henri Cartier-Bresson down there on the Square with his Leica, stopping suddenly to nab the Decisive Moment.

—8/21/97

Secret Agents

In 1907 the great Polish-born author Joseph Conrad wrote a novel called *The Secret Agent*. Supposedly based on an unsolved terrorist bombing, it's the story of Verloc, a nervous London shopkeeper who's working as an agent for a European embassy bent on neutralizing the anarchists. The embassy wishes to outrage complacent London society by staging an anarchist-style attack: that is, by bombing a target chosen for its senselessness.

The target Mr. Vladimir and Mr. Verloc choose is the Greenwich Observatory, where people go to look at the stars. Any other target would appear to have a too-specific political motive. The Greenwich Observatory is just senseless enough. Verloc himself is reluctant. As it happens, the only "secret agent" bold enough to place the bomb is Mr. Verloc's innocent, retarded brother-in-law, Stevie. He means well, but on the way, Stevie trips on a root. He's "blown to small bits—limbs, gravel, clothing, bones, splinters—all mixed together."

The plot replays itself frequently in the Middle East, but no one ever learns from its irony. There are still a lot of Stevies in the world.

Contrary to what all the talking heads say, terrorism is not new to America. It's definitely not new to the Southeast.

A mysterious package with a time bomb goes off late at night, injuring several innocent citizens. "I can't understand it," one appalled victim says. "We're living in the United States."

Those words are spoken in Clinton, Tennessee, in 1957. Late one night, a two-toned late-model car drives into a black residential neighborhood. A white man in khakis gets out of his car and places a suitcase beside the road, near several houses and a restaurant, then drives away. Minutes later, the suitcase explodes, destroying the restaurant and a family home, demolishing two cars, and damaging about 30 other houses. Among the injured is an 11-month-old baby, hit in the forehead by flying glass.

Days later, at Knoxville's Chilhowee Park, a Louis Armstrong concert is briefly interrupted by a dynamite bomb that explodes outside the auditorium. In all, there are at least a dozen bombings in and around Clinton over a period of about two years, all of them tied to segregationist resistance to a plan to make Clinton High one of the South's first high schools to desegregate.

In the early fall of 1958, three powerful bombs go off in the middle of the night, blowing apart most of Clinton High School, the focus of the controversy. The FBI investigates.

Implicated, and blamed by many, was a very unusual young man named John Kasper. Raised in New Jersey, Kasper was a fixture in New York's Greenwich Village during the days of beat and bebop. In his early 20s, he opened a Village bookstore he called "Make It New," inspired by a line from poet Ezra Pound, the radical poet of the Lost Generation. Biracial audiences would sit on the floor of Kasper's shop and talk poetry and jazz, which Kasper loved. He impressed some visitors as a man well versed in black culture.

Kasper especially loved Ezra Pound, who was then institutionalized in St. Elizabeth's mental hospital in Washington, D.C. Pound had been imprisoned by American troops in 1945 for his pro-fascist propaganda during the war. Kasper soon moved to Washington, opened another bookstore, befriended Pound, and frequently visited the elderly poet. Kasper's friends complained that suddenly he had no time for anyone else.

Pound was then hard at work on his *Cantos*, the lengthy and indecipherable multilingual poem that he never finished writing. Kasper testified on Pound's behalf before a Senate subcommittee in early 1956, calling Pound a "political prisoner ... one of the highest world intelligences." Kasper proceeded to indict the whole study of psychiatry as a Zionist conspiracy.

Months later John Kasper was in Clinton. Forty years ago this summer, he was strolling around white Clinton neighborhoods showing baffled residents photographs of black men kissing white women, telling them that's what's going to happen if you let Clinton High desegregate.

Desegregation was a Communist plot, he declared, intent on ruining the white American race through interbreeding.

Most Clintonians, who didn't care that much for Yankees to begin with, didn't buy it. Aided by Alabama segregationist Ace Carter, however, Kasper became local leader of the White Citizens Council, a small but active group of segregationists who provoked a riot at the school at the beginning of its first integrated year. A white Baptist minister who'd escorted black students was attacked and beaten by a mob of men and women.

But Clinton voters ignored the slate of segregationist candidates in the election that year. Most East Tennesseans were disgusted by Kasper's methods. You get the feeling that some would-be segregationists may have become desegregationists when they witnessed the tactics of the White Citizens Council.

Annoyed Clinton deputies arrested Kasper for sedition and inciting to riot. They couldn't make it stick at first, but finally an all-white Knoxville jury under Judge Robert Love Taylor (nephew of Fiddlin' Bob) convicted Kasper of conspiracy to resist a Supreme Court ruling, Brown vs. Board of Education. The jury also convicted six locals, all of them, curiously, much older than their leader, John Kasper. Judge Taylor blamed Kasper chiefly, declaring that the six wouldn't have made trouble if not for Kasper's influence.

He got only a year. Neither Kasper nor anyone else was ever found guilty of the Clinton and Knoxville bombings. Reading about Kasper and his obsessions, you might get the uneasy suspicion the whole noisy mess was Ezra Pound's idea. Pound's old pal Ernest Hemingway tried to persuade the 73-year-old poet to repudiate Kasper, and disavow the Tennessee bombings. Pound refused. Somehow, though, Pound gained release from the asylum and quickly made his way back to Italy, where he spent the rest of his life.

Fortunately, no one was killed or seriously injured in the local bombings. But years later, when another bomb killed four Sunday-school children in Alabama, segregationists seemed to lose their rhetorical flourish.

John Kasper was nuts. The case of this jazz hound from Greenwich Village fretting about racial mixing at Clinton High is one for psychologists, Zionist conspirators though they might be. Trying to make sense of terrorism may be the first mistake in trying to understand it.

—8/1/96

JACK NEELY

CHAPTER THREE

SPIRITS

The Residence of a Poet

During Andrew Jackson's first term in the White House, America was a country known for its politics, not its literature. Poe was in his early 20s, unknown but for some slim volumes of poetry. Hawthorne was unpublished. Melville, Whitman—they were just kids.

But out here on the frontier, something was stirring. In 1831 an intellectual club called the Knoxville Lyceum planned lectures and organized a library. The same year local printer Frederick Heiskell dipped a toe into the literary current by publishing a Knoxville edition of Oliver Goldsmith's witty novel *The Vicar of Wakefield*.

Then, on July 9, 1832, an anxious young man named Charles Todd carried a freshly printed book into the Knoxville office of the District Clerk to register a copyright. With Heiskell's help, Todd had just done something no other Tennessean had ever done. He'd published a novel.

Woodville was an unusual piece of work. Following the fashion of the day, it bore an alternate title, *The Anchoret Reclaimed*—just in case you didn't like the first one.

Lord Byron, dead eight years earlier, haunts the book in quotes and allusions. Byron once claimed that "truth is stranger than fiction." *Woodville* is a little stranger than either one. A strong romantic brew of despair, murder, and always-stormy skies, the novel follows the career of a moody fellow named Allison Woodville, whom we meet living in the woods with Ned, an elderly slave—and a "huge spaniel" named Trajan, to whom Woodville occasionally writes sonnets.

Poor Woodville, we learn later, had been smitten with a beautiful woman named Matilda, whose mother disapproved of the unlanded eccentric. When Matilda marries a twit named Hanson, Woodville bolts for Europe—where, like Byron, he gets passionately involved in the Greek revolution. Naturally, there he happens to encounter his Smoky Mountain nemesis, Hanson, just after the battle of Karpanitza, and kills him in a pistol duel. Woodville flees home—only to discover, soon after his arrival, that by a tangle of revealed relationships, the woman he'd been in love with was really his *sister*!

Aieee! That explains why we find Woodville living in the woods, writing sonnets to a dog.

Actually, the local action takes place in an unnamed state in the Southern mountains. Todd mentions some "towns:" S—, L—, and R—, none readily recognizable. If I'm ever institutionalized, the first thing I'll do is spread out a map and figure it all out. In his preface Todd explains that because his tale, "related to me under peculiar circumstances," was mainly true, he felt obliged to "disguise the characters and incidents...in order to elude detection."

By the way, in this pioneering American novel, Woodville's most loyal friend (besides the dog) is a character with the unlikely name of Hemingway.

At his best, Todd sounds something like Poe soon would—like when he describes "a mind...emerging from that thraldom of wretchedness which the world's depravity imposes." But Todd was different from Poe in one respect: Poe and most others tended to set their fiction in distant times or exotic locations, convinced that modern America couldn't quite bear the load of real passion. Most of Todd's story is contemporary, and local.

As Woodville and Matilda read Byron together in the mountains, Woodville exclaims, "What a charming place it would be for the residence of a poet!" But the practical Matilda responds, "I think there are perhaps but few poets who could content themselves to reside in so remote a region." If *Woodville* has any literary significance today, it might be for that attempt to clear a literary landscape in America.

A week after Todd released the text, the hard-core Democratic *Knoxville Register* raved about it: "The story is interesting, the style good," the blurb went "...and provided it had been composed in England and praised by the reviewers, it would be a great book." Knoxville had a chip on its shoulder even 162 years ago.

The author himself remains a more shadowy character than Woodville. He was said to be a former professor at Maryville College, but nobody really knows who he was. Soon after *Woodville*, Todd was facing a murder charge; the specifics, including the victims and the verdict, are lost to history. Then Charles Todd drops out of the histories of Knoxville and American literature altogether.

Like one of his moody characters, in his preface Todd confesses "a depressing fear of a failure." Poignantly he adds that he is "cheered with the animating hope that it will meet the smiles of a generous and enlightened community, as being the harbinger of better things."

Mr. Todd, wherever you are, I hope you're right

— 5/20/94

All Dreaming

Singer Natalie Merchant's solo album, out just this year, is called *Tigerlily*. Natalie seems like a reader, but I doubt she ever read a novel called *Tiger-Lilies*, even though it got written up in the big magazines.

Picture this: Upon getting off the train in downtown Knoxville, a whimsical young German lady named Ottilie resolves to change her wardrobe. Surveying the horizon, Ottilie exclaims to her servant, in German: "Yonder are the mountains—they look lonely. I yearn to plunge myself into that blue ocean of loneliness over yonder. What a color is blue, Gretchen! I will wear it hereafter. The sea is blue, the mountains are blue, the heavens are blue. One might think blue was good for sick souls as for weak eyes."

The writer who introduced these ladies to Knoxville, you might have guessed from reading that passage, was no novelist. He was, however, regarded as the South's finest poet of his era: the skinny, tubercular, tetched Georgian Sidney Lanier. He wrote the book during the Civil War under rather trying circumstances.

Had not Poe beat him to it, Lanier might have single-handedly invented the myth of the Romantic Southern Poet. Like Poe, he had a bad experience in the military, struggled with poverty, worshipped women, coughed a lot, and wrote some lovely verse. He was dead by 40, as all Romantic Southern Poets must be, of the poet's disease, consumption, the same bug that killed Keats—the English poet whom Lanier quotes at length in *Tiger-Lilies*.

Lanier was from Georgia but spent some of his fondest days hereabouts. He was a teenager when his family bought (and named) the Lamar House on Gay Street, a little older when the Laniers bought a country hotel called Montvale Springs, in the foothills of Blount County—where you can still see the ruins of an old resort, the stone steps leading to nowhere, now the centerpiece of a YMCA camp.

"The seven-gabled hotel at Montvale" in 1860 where Sidney Lanier spent the summer when he was 18—what may have been the last untroubled time of his life—became the basis for some of his very best poetry as well as one of the 19th century's strangest novels.

In *Tiger-Lilies*, Ottilie and Gretchen get off the train at the old station and get a horse-drawn cab to the hotel. In those days Gay Street was a steep uphill climb from what's now the Southern station. ("The road from the Knoxville depot into the city is a perilous one," Lanier writes.) Their horseman has trouble with the horses, which balk and rear, almost tumbling their coach down the steep embankment. Suddenly a tall, mysterious Cherokee in a slouch hat and moccasins appears, seizes the bridles, and quiets the horses, saving the ladies.

Ottilie tries to tip the "majestic, brawny man." He declines but offers to accompany them. "I will go with you, Fraulein," says the Indian, "anywhere." His name is Jim Saggs, but the whimsical Ottilie insists on calling him *Chilhowee*—because, she says, "I like good names."

That brief Knoxville scene is mere prelude to a bizarre conclave in the mountains, mainly in the ballroom at Montvale Springs. A group of bohemian revelers, allegedly including Lanier himself, dress in costume as Mark Antony, Francisco Pizarro, King Arthur, and Greek Naiads.

Drinking champagne and talking about Egypt, a woman fashions a pyramid hat out of bran. A prankster-clown ties the current issue of *Brownlow's Whig* to Satan's pointed tail. "Life! Life! Down with Death!" Pizarro shouts. There's a formal French duel with rapiers. They argue about pantheism and smokers' rights and arrange a Chopin orchestral piece for voices. One concludes that "Beethoven is to Chopin as a wild mountain is to a flower growing on it."

The whole thing might seem pretty silly—until you remember that Lanier wrote the East Tennessee scenes between deadly fevers as a blockade-runner in the Confederate Navy and as a POW in a Northern prison camp.

The *Atlantic Monthly* didn't cut him much slack, though. "*Tiger-Lilies* will not do," their reviewer concluded in 1868. The book sold not quite 1,000 copies and has been out of print for most of the 127 years since. Today it's read mainly by eccentric professors. But even the *Atlantic* admitted that it held "some original poetry." The novel's East Tennessee section ends with this passage at the estate of the imagination they call Thalberg House, at night: "not quiet, being full of young and passionate hearts of men and women, some sleeping, some waking, all dreaming."

—12/7/95

The Republican Id

This year, like every second year, you'll hear about the Knoxville district's unbroken chain of Republican representatives going back to the Civil War. It's a record of party consistency that's extremely unusual, maybe unique, in American politics.

It's inevitable, they say, this primordial juggernaut that started back before the telephone and the light bulb and the automobile. There's no use in resisting it. It will forever be so.

The Republican Party, born as the civil-rights, big-government party, has changed in nearly every respect since the Civil War. The only thing that's remained consistent about the Republican Party in America may be its hold on Tennessee's Second District. Surely there is some meaning in that fact.

But what is it, exactly, that we're hanging on to, that we've loyally remembered every 24 months since Union occupation? To get at the heart of this phenomenon, we need to examine the exotic origin of the Republican Second District.

The Abraham of this Birthright was an Ivy-Leaguer from up North. Tall, dark-skinned, with Asiatic features, he wore his hair unfashionably long, as if to feed the rumors that he was an Indian. He also wore a black goatee. He was especially popular with the ladies. A self-styled intellectual, as a young man he co-founded the *Junto*, one of Knoxville's first literary salons, and under an odd pseudonym wrote sarcastic essays ridiculing conventional life.

And, of course, he was a big-government liberal, as most Republicans were in those days. In fact, he was famously radical. If he was not the sort of person you picture when you think of a multi-term Second District Republican representative, he's also not the sort you picture when you hear a name like Horace Maynard.

Around here, he was known as "the Narragansett." The teenagers at the college on the Hill began calling him that after one remarked, the day he arrived, that he resembled "an Injun." That was in 1838, the year Horace Maynard, the valedictorian at Amherst College, arrived in Knoxville, following his Amherst pal Perez Dickinson (cousin of Emily). Maynard took a job at the college, teaching math and ancient languages.

Some say Horace Maynard acknowledged his Indian background but corrected it as Algonquin, not Narragansett. He was also allegedly descended from a proud old English family but for some reason prohibited his family from displaying the Maynard crest.

At 26 or so he began writing diatribes for the *Knoxville Times* under the curious name Zadoc Jones. Several were assaults on the complacent middle class: "I esteem the herd of mankind, the human cattle, no better than other cattle, nor quite so good," Maynard wrote, as Zadoc.

At first, Knoxvillians found the nonconformist Yankee off-putting: sarcastic, chilly, sometimes belligerent. But he became one of Tennessee's most popular speakers, known for his energetic style, jabbing an index finger into the air to make a point. (Maynard once jabbed a Democratic editor with a cane to make another sort of point.)

Maynard left academia to go into law, then left law to go into politics. In his 30s, he was a presidential elector for the Whig ticket, and was elected to Congress as a Whig in 1857. When secession was in the air, he canvassed his district, desperately seeking votes to keep Tennessee in the Union, braving secessionist assassins. A longtime member of the Second Presbyterian Church, Maynard was absent when his old friend and preacher, the pro-Confederate Rev. Martin, publicly prayed that Maynard be banished from Tennessee and that his "bones shall bleach upon the Cumberland Mountains." Maynard's wife and children took offense and left the service.

Exiled in the capital, during the War Horace Maynard was the only congressional representative from Tennessee of any party. Maynard befriended President Lincoln and was soon calling himself a Republican. But Maynard thought Lincoln's reconstruction plans too forgiving toward the Confederate traitors. He sided with the vengeful Radicals and made enemies nationwide. A Cincinnati paper declared him to be "the meanest man in American politics."

In 1875 President Grant appointed Maynard U.S. Minister to Turkey, a job he apparently accepted with some gusto. On the way, he formally and enthusiastically met Queen Victoria. To greet the queen, Horace Maynard of Henley Street wore satin knee breeches, black stockings, patent-leather pumps, and a sword.

He arrived in Constantinople that summer and commenced what sounds like the time of his life. He made friends with the sultan, who declared Maynard an "American dervish." He sparred with the Grand Vizier. He enjoyed the fireworks along the Bosphorus (especially for the sultan's birthday). He developed a taste for "coffee a la Turque"—as his wife enjoyed Turkish bonbons. Minister Maynard assisted Schliemann's famous excavation of Troy and, from another friend, obtained a chunk of the ancient Greek Temple of Apollo to bring with him back to Knoxville. For all I know, it may be knocking around here somewhere. Be careful what you throw out.

At home the Democratic dailies, enviously playing off Maynard's old ladies'-man reputation, charged that the former representative was sultan of a Turkish harem.

Not ready to retire at 66, Maynard returned stateside for a spell as U.S. postmaster general, then retired to Knoxville. The globetrotting

Narragansett died in his old home at the corner of Main and Henley. His funeral parade was 60 carriages long and his burial, near the gate at Old Gray on Broadway, was witnessed by an estimated 10,000. Maynardville, Tennessee, was named in his honor.

He was not quite 68 when he died. Had Horace Maynard made it past 180, he still would never have seen a non-Republican warming his old seat in Congress.

If you find yourself tiring of your Second District Republican representative, try to read between the lines of his legislative updates and remember that somewhere deep inside, maybe, there's a longhaired, coffee-drinking, stocking-wearing, hot-blooded half-breed nonconformist radical—a sort of Republican Id, named Zadoc Jones.

—8/15/96

Tear It Up, Boys

The man who'd called that meeting at Star Billiards was uncommonly fair-minded for a guy who lived in Knoxville in 1865. The War was allegedly over, but Knoxville that summer would see lynchings of men whose main fault was that they'd been on the Other Side during the late unpleasantness. But the dozens of guys who crowded the billiard saloon on Gay between Church and Cumberland weren't picking fights or telling war stories; they were talking about something much newer to the South than bloodshed, an unusual sport called baseball.

It was the idea of a clerk who worked for the local federal revenue office, a young Union veteran named Samuel B. Dow. "The boys whom I picked to attend were both Northerners and Southerners," Dow said, "since it was my idea to pick the best team possible regardless of their position in the late war."

Dow had invited about 60 men to try out for what he believed to be the South's first organized baseball team. (Maybe it wasn't that—there'd apparently been some baseball in New Orleans just before the War—but still, it was mighty early.)

Surveying the throng that showed up at Star Billiards that day, Dow was quick to notice something peculiar. Not one of the former Confederates he'd invited had shown up.

Dow and his pals shrugged, named themselves "The Knoxvilles," and made plans to play ball. The first order of business was to find a place. On the north end of the business district, at the bottom of a steep hill below Gay Street, was a vacant, tolerably flat spot. It would later be known as the 400 block, but in 1865 it was the town dump. To Dow it was the obvious place to introduce baseball to Tennessee, with a hill that would make "natural bleachers." With permission from the owners of the lot, the aspiring baseballers met there, cleared the trash, mowed the cockleburs and jimson weeds, and made a baseball diamond.

Dow didn't know it yet, but the Rebels who didn't show at Star Billiards that day had plans of their own. Along with a couple of errant Unionists, they formed a team called the Holstons, including assistant postmaster Samuel Luttrell and, significantly, a former Confederate messenger named William Caswell. The Holstons cleared a lot on Jackson Avenue and began practicing for the obvious confrontation.

The town closed down; Dow's "natural bleachers" filled to overflowing. A brass band heralded the first baseball game in regional history. Home plate was exactly where the brewpub is now.

It started, predictably, with a legal argument. Bob Armstrong, of the Holstons, protested that two "Knoxvilles" had just moved here and weren't in his mind bona fide Knoxvillians. They ironed out the eligibility issue somehow, and then they played ball.

Baseball, as played by guys who'd just gotten home from the bloodiest war in American history, was a little different from what we know today. There were no hats with visors, no gloves, and bats were homemade wooden clubs that were four or five feet long. It was a dangerous game.

The first injury came in the first inning, when the Knoxvilles' outfielder, Spencer Munson, broke his arm while fielding a fly; the bone cracking was audible across the field. In the second inning, another Holston drove a "hot liner" straight back at Dow, the pitcher, snapping his right middle finger backwards. With his finger hanging useless, Dow "managed to pitch out the inning." Dow was later persuaded to retire to play third base, while attorney and former Union Major Eldad Cicero Camp replaced him on the mound.

But Major Camp—the same guy who later shot a former Confederate officer to death on Walnut Street—was no pitcher. "The Holstons began to hit his offerings all over...Gay, Jackson, and State Streets," Dow later recalled. That third inning, things were looking very bad for the partially disabled Knoxvilles. They got their revenge later in the game when Bill Chamberlain hit a pop fly to center field. The outfielder lost the ball in the sun's glare; it plummeted through his bare hands and struck him right between the eyes, knocking him cold. An ambulance carried the luckless Holston off the field. The Knoxvilles won the game by 17 runs.

The Holstons won some future matches. One particularly worthy Holston, aptly named Tim Homer, hit the longest home run ever confirmed—out of the park to the 200 block of Gay, about where the Treble Clef monument is now. All the baserunners were relaxing on the bench by the time center-fielder Chamberlain returned with the ball.

However, Dow himself, who wielded the largest bat anyone had seen, hit one ball that some swore was headed right toward the railroad station, a couple of blocks past Homer's mark. It was never found.

The Knoxvilles would play other fledgling teams from around the region: Chattanooga, Greenville, Atlanta. Local businessmen made extravagant bets on games, sometimes in the hundreds of dollars, sometimes even wagering houses and yards. After a hotly contested win over Greenville, ecstatic revelers knocked the tall silk hat off the head of one lucky investor named Cyrus Zimmerman and began kicking it around. Zimmerman wasn't upset. "Tear it up, boys," he said. "I can buy a lot more of them now."

Around 1870, though, the drug company known as Sanford, Chamberlain & Albers put up a building right on the diamond, and the team had to find other quarters.

A half-century after that original game, former barehanded Holstons star William Caswell, now a wealthy old man, donated a park near downtown for the enjoyment of what was, for at least 70 years, Knoxville's most popular sport. I'm planning to see a game there this weekend, in fact, the Smokies vs. ancient rival Chattanooga—but I'm no nostalgist. I'm taking a glove.

—5/22/97

Active Service

For the past four years we've all been annoyed to hear questions about whether Atlanta's too small and unsophisticated to support the Olympic

Games. "What does Atlanta have to do with the Olympics," they asked.

Knoxville is much smaller and perhaps less sophisticated than Atlanta. Still, experience has proven to me that if you look back far enough, danged if you won't find a Knoxvillian behind nearly everything, good and bad.

Cherchez le Knoxvillien is my motto. Surely there's a Knoxville-Olympic link, somewhere, that predates even the Lady Vols.

When I heard rumors that there's an elderly Olympian fencer of one of the most dramatic early Games living quietly here in Knoxville, I tracked him down—but was disappointed to learn he wants nothing to do with reporters, perhaps wisely. So to find *le Knoxvillien*, I looked even further back in Olympic history—to the very first one, a century ago. As we should have known, the modern Olympic Games have Knoxville fingerprints on them.

They belong to a man born on the highest hill in downtown Knoxville, a decade before the Civil War. Son of a local judge, Ebenezer Alexander grew up with a classical Greek last name in Civil War-era Knoxville. Orphaned by 15, Alexander enrolled in the university's prep program when old Union trenches still gathered rain on the Hill and the main building bore the scars of Confederate cannonballs. There he grew fascinated with all things Greek and studied well, well enough to get into Yale.

He returned to Knoxville after graduation, intended to go into law, but quickly tired of it. Then UT offered him a job as a classics instructor; by the time he was 26, he was a full professor. He married a local girl, had some kids, and settled in at his home on Temple, near campus, for the next 13 years. Quiet, soft-spoken, slow to anger, he became what a newspaper editor later called the "most popular man who ever lived in Knox County." He was one of Lawson McGhee Library's original trustees. Elected chairman of UT's faculty, Alexander was discussed as a likely prospect for university president. But at 35, he was uncomfortable with UT's campaign to de-emphasize the classics in favor of engineering and practical sciences. UNC called, and the mustachioed professor moved to Chapel Hill to teach Greek.

Seven years later President Cleveland, needing a fluent Greek speaker with social skills, appointed Alexander Minister to Greece, Rumania, and Serbia. In 1893 Alexander moved to Athens and became a "favorite" with the Greek royal family, including King George and Crown Prince Constantine. He also befriended the young American correspondent/novelist Stephen Crane and his companion, Cora, an errant wife and former madame. She later recalled Alexander's unusual kindness toward the unconventional couple. Crane modeled a character after Alexander in his novel *Active Service* and dedicated the book to him.

And there in Athens, Alexander became part of the gathering Olympic movement—a thrill to any scholar of ancient Greece, these competitions held for the first time in more than 1,500 years, with their homage to Marathon and the tragedy of Phidippides.

In 1895 *Harper's* magazine reported that Alexander was the very first to donate money to the Olympic project—some thought it remarkable that the first donor was an American, not a European—but that wasn't likely Alexander's most important contribution. The Olympics faced political opposition from several quarters, even within Greece. Alexander helped grease the diplomatic wheels to give this extremely unusual international event an unlikely peaceful start. Some sources suggest he was also decisive in bringing his own country's best there, recruiting America to be part of this unlikely experiment from the very beginning.

The United States was one of only 13 nations competing in the 1896 Games. And the U.S. sent only 13 guys in all, most of whom participated in more than one event. The 45-year-old Alexander befriended the first American Olympians and did his best to acquaint them with Greece and its mysterious language.

As the U.S. Minister rooted for them in the stadium at the very first modern Olympics, the Americans dominated the track and field events. Even with Professor Alexander promoting it, however, the original Olympics got little attention in the Knoxville papers, the American winners dutifully listed in the back pages. Attended by 60,000 (mostly Greeks), the Marathon got slight emphasis in the Knoxville *Journal*, under the headline "Ancient Athletics." In 1896 the regional horse races at Montgomery Park in Memphis, the "Tennessee Brewery Stakes," made a much bigger sports story.

Alexander returned to Chapel Hill and became dean of UNC. But he frequently returned to Knoxville to see friends and family—his son, also named Ebenezer, was gaining a reputation as a local surgeon—and to give an occasional lecture on the classics. He was commencement speaker here in 1898. In ill health, Alexander returned to Knoxville in 1909. Two days after his 59th birthday, on a chilly Friday evening in early March, 1910, the former Athenian alighted from his coach at Brown and McCulla Livery Stable, at the corner of Market and Church (it has survived into the automobile era as the Pryor-Brown Garage). He'd hardly touched the pavement before he collapsed. He died soon afterward.

Knoxville spent the weekend mourning Alexander's death and buried him at Old Gray on Broadway in the city where, despite his travels, he spent most of his life.

By that time there'd been three other Olympic Games since the original one in Athens, all of them smeared with political, personal, and technical problems. Some described St. Louis in 1904 as a "fiasco." By 1908, most of the world's nations weren't yet participating. The torch, the theme music, the five-ring logo were all yet to come. The Stockholm Games, which, with the help of Jim Thorpe caught the world's imagination as no other games had, were still two years off.

Chances are, the evening he died in downtown Knoxville, Ebenezer Alexander had never guessed the magnitude of the ancient spirit he'd helped summon back to the living world.

—7/18/96

Alexander the Great

A year-and-a-half ago, I wrote a column about Ebenezer Alexander (1851-1910), the Knoxville-raised classics professor who, if he wasn't exactly the Father of the Modern Olympics, was at least the Uncle.

He's buried in Old Gray beneath a ponderous granite stone that's carved TEACHER ADMINISTRATOR DIPLOMAT.

When I wrote that story during the 1996 Summer Games, I didn't expect to get a call from the statesman's grandson. Ebenezer Alexander bears the name of his father and grandfather and a few others before that. (He thinks he's the 7th, and goes by *Eben*, as most modern Ebenezers do.) At 85 he's a neurologist, still on the teaching staff at Wake Forest University, still an influential consultant on the board of a few neurological journals.

He hasn't lived in Knoxville since 1926 and has mixed memories of the place. His family lived near UT, in the neighborhood where his grandfather had lived as a UT professor half a century earlier. His parents enrolled him in dance classes; he preferred football. He recalls the neighborhood team he joined, circa 1925: the Circle Park Juniors, they called themselves. Alexander remembers the team posing for a photograph on the rock in Circle Park where they played, long before the park had anything to do with a university campus.

He remembers the pre-TVA floods and the big logs and dead horses that would drift through Knoxville afterward. "Knoxville was a *dirty* city," he says. "You knew if you wore a white shirt and went downtown, you'd come back with streaks of black on it. You'd have to blow your nose to get it all cleared out. And it was not a well-run city; there was a lot of crookery."

Alexander's parents shipped him off to McCallie when he was 13; after that, he returned only to visit. But he enjoys those visits and likes Knoxville much better now than he did when he was 12. "Knoxville's one of the most improved cities in America," he says. "Pittsburgh included."

Ambassador Alexander died three years before neurosurgeon Alexander was born, but Dr. Alexander spent much of his youth in the company of his grandfather's spirit. When he attended UNC around 1930, his grandfather remained a formidable presence there. The younger Alexander took Greek from an idolatrous former student of his grandfather's. "It was almost overbearing," Dr. Alexander recalls, "how monumental he was" at UNC, even 20 years after his death. The ambassador was known, among other things, for his courtly habits. Sitting on his front porch as a lady strolled by, he'd stand and tip his hat. Once when he observed a student chewing tobacco on the back row and spitting on the floor, the professor-diplomat quietly drew out a clean handkerchief and mopped it up.

Professor Alexander was small and thin, sometimes frail, and smoked a pipe. Dr. Alexander doesn't think his grandfather was ever a competitive athlete. Still, he could perform some remarkable physical feats. At least twice the professor *walked* all the way from Chapel Hill to Knoxville, camping with Cherokees along the way. According to family legend, Alexander was so nimble, he could walk down a dusty road without raising enough of a cloud to get his trousers dirty.

JACK NEELY

Once Dr. Alexander opened a bureau owned by his grandfather. "The smell of pipe tobacco was very pungent," he says. Dr. Alexander's father, a respected local surgeon, blamed tobacco for his diplomat father's sudden death of a heart attack in downtown Knoxville. The younger Dr. Alexander is skeptical, believing it was the result of the congenital heart irregularity he suffered himself at the same age. A pacemaker, he thinks, might have saved his grandfather.

If his family knew Ebenezer Alexander's contribution to the modern Olympics, they didn't brag to the kids. "Even when I was growing up, the Olympics just weren't all that big," Dr. Alexander says. Most of what he knows about his grandfather he's learned through his own research.

Most of the participants in the first Olympic Games were Europeans recruited by the French Baron de Coubertin; pragmatic Americans had to be convinced. "Coubertin contacted my grandfather because he was the U.S. ambassador," says Dr. Alexander. "He thought it was the best bet to get the Americans involved." Alexander put the word out, and a group of Ivy League athletes organized a team and came to Greece. The Americans' presence made the Olympics seem much more like a world event, not just another quaint European conceit.

"None of them knew what the hell they were doing," Dr. Alexander says of the first American Olympians. "They practiced in the nude because they'd seen these ancient vases depicting nude athletes." After their arrival in Greece, they were told they could wear clothes.

Ambassador Alexander kept them out of trouble. "Somebody said he even gave every one of them a pistol, to protect themselves," Dr. Alexander says. "There was a lot of skullduggery over there. I don't know whether that story's true or not."

Alexander affirms that his grandfather was close friends with the novelist Stephen Crane, who then lived in Athens and modeled a character in his novel *Active Service* after Alexander. Dr. Alexander has a copy Crane inscribed to his grandfather.

Dr. Alexander regrets one thing about his grandfather's 1893-97 ambassadorship: "He didn't get the Bosnia situation straightened out." For Ebenezer Alexander, that might have taken another year or two.

—2/19/98

Seeking Grace

Fifty years ago this Sunday, a DC-3 took off from a Copenhagen airport, ascended too sharply into a strong headwind, and plummeted to the ground, killing all 19 aboard. Among the dead was Gustav, the crown prince of Sweden. Another was Scandinavian movie starlet Gerda Newman. Also killed was one American, a 48-year-old woman from Jellico named Grace Moore.

Her career had been unprecedented: headliner in Broadway musicals, diva of the Metropolitan Opera, movie star. Her 1934 movie *One Night of Love*, regarded as the first Hollywood musical with decent music, was nominated for an academy award for Best Picture (Moore herself was one of only three nominees for Best Actress). The film told the story of a spirited American opera singer: Grace Moore's biography in romantic disguise.

She made several other movies and, without losing credibility, returned to the opera. Some critics commented that it was not her natural talent or discipline, but just her sheer force of will that smoothed her path to success.

The Harlequin Romance people would reject Grace Moore's story as implausible. She dated Maurice Chevalier and George Gershwin, drank with Cole Porter and Scott and Zelda Fitzgerald, worked with Irving Berlin and Jascha Heifetz. In 1932 Florenz Ziegfeld declared the blonde diva from Jellico was one of the 10 most beautiful women in the world.

Not too shabby for anybody, never mind one born in rural Cocke County in 1898; throughout a marriage and advice that she pick a glamorous Italian stage name like *Graziana Moroni,* she kept her birth name, if not her birthdate (some Hollywood sources have her born in 1900 or 1901). She grew up mostly in Jellico, where today a local restaurant's menu welcomes us to the *Home of Grace Moore.*

Back when freeway cloverleafs had proper names, the one in downtown Knoxville was famous as the *Grace Moore Cloverleaf.* She'd lived here, too, and not far from that site.

Grace Moore's capsule bios don't mention Knoxville. Her longer biographies—including the one she wrote herself, apologizing for not waiting for old age—offer little about her life here. By her own account, her preschool childhood was a Heidi-like idyll of romping with horses among the green hills of the Cocke County countryside, washing clothes in the creek with homemade soap.

Moore's lively autobiography recalls moving to Knoxville at the age of 5 as a traumatic change for this country girl. "I hated my new city clothes and the awful city shoes—the first I had ever worn." She said mean kindergarten kids made fun of her accent and overstarched dress. (You could write a thesis about Knoxville kids ridiculing country kids who would one day overshadow them.)

"Knoxville was only an interlude, for we soon moved again," she recalled.

The Knoxville City Directory, however, betrays some interesting inconsistencies—and maybe some clues. According to her own account and a later full-length biography by a Grace Moore scholar, the Moores moved to Knoxville as Grace turned 5—which would have been late 1903—and stayed only a few months.

But the name of Grace's father, Richard L. Moore, first appears here in 1900, when he was a salesman living on Morgan Street, a working-class neighborhood near the freightyards on the north side of downtown. The Moores' 1900 census form, on which they listed their 1-year-old girl as "Gracie," confirms it: during her early childhood, Grace Moore lived not in pastoral Cocke County but in smoky, crowded, industrial Knoxville. And they apparently lived here for years.

When Grace was about 3, according to the city directory, the Moores moved to a rental house on Florida Street. A scrap of it's still there, just east of the Old City, parallel to Central. It's now a gray, industrial couple of blocks of loading docks and Hurricane fences.

But the street where Mrs. Moore so carefully starched her 5-year-old daughter's dresses was then a residential street—and one of Knoxville's most dangerous neighborhoods. From about 1900 to about 1914, encompassing the Moores' stay there, Florida Street had a special designation with the city authorities. It was Knoxville's red-light district. Liberal Mayor Heiskell specifically designated Florida Street as a sort of urban experiment where prostitutes could ply their trade unharrassed. It became known as "Friendly Town."

The Moores lived on the northern part of Florida Street, near Fifth

Avenue—about where Harrison's Chicken City is now. On a rise uphill from most of Florida, their own block may have been a little cleaner, quieter, safer than the rest of Florida Street: a mixed block of pharmacists and pool-hall proprietors. (This leg of Florida was later renamed Randolph Street, the name it goes by now, maybe to distinguish it from the more notorious blocks of Florida Street.) Still, for four years, most of their time in Knoxville, the Moores lived within sight of East Tennessee's highest concentration of brothels, gambling dens, and often-violent saloons. If little Grace Moore had bounced a ball in her front yard, it might have rolled past more than one whorehouse.

By the time she was 8 or so, she was in Jellico and, by all accounts, a remarkable child, better known for her astonishing will than for her voice. (One day she took it as her duty to free all the horses enslaved in downtown Jellico; another day she was accused of theft. And when you hear sweet old ladies say, "Girls just didn't play basketball in my day," smile and nod politely, but don't believe them. Grace Moore was a basketball star in Jellico, captain of her high school team, in 1915.)

After about a decade in Jellico and a misadventure at Nashville's Ward Belmont School, Grace Moore was singing in New York's Black Cat Cafe, turning heads, well on her way.

When she told her life story for publication, Grace Moore may have condensed her several Knoxville years to make that Hollywood birthdate math work out right. Considering she offered so little about her urban youth, we can only guess about her impression of the ladies loitering on the sidewalk down Florida Street. But you can't help but wonder if it might have given this 6- or 7-year-old a special fear of failure, a dread that matured into the indomitable will that would astonish opera critics at the Met.

—1/23/97

The Finest Journalist

When you think of Knoxvillians who've won Pulitzer Prizes, you think of two: Knoxville native James Agee, whose A Death in the Family won the Pulitzer for literature; and Don Whitehead, the war correspondent who won two reporting Pulitzers, then retired to become a gentleman columnist in Knoxville.

JACK NEELY

But the one Pulitzer laureate we never, ever hear about is arguably the one who was most indelibly formed by Knoxville. Legendary newspaperman Heywood Broun called him "drunk or sober...the finest journalist of his day." His obscurity in his hometown may have something to do with the manner of his early death.

In South Knoxville, in the graveyard of the Island Home Baptist Church, are modest graves clustered in family plots. It looks like any semi-rural Baptist churchyard, full of unpretentious gravestones, some handmade, some even misspelled. But one especially tall stone can startle you. Engraved there is a line unlike any other in Tennessee: *AWARDED THE PULITZER PRIZE IN JOURNALISM IN 1929.* At the top, under an engraved art-deco lantern, is the name *PAUL Y. ANDERSON.*

He grew up not far from this churchyard, a short walk out Sevierville Pike. His father, Holston Anderson, was a stonecutter. In the winter of 1897, when he was not quite 40, Holston Anderson was working in W.C. Doyle's stone quarry down on the Hiwassee, cutting out big rocks for the piers of the new Knox County bridge. He'd just finished with one when the derrick broke and fell on him.

Paul was only three and a half. They say the early death of Holston Anderson infected his boy with a bitterness that would scare Mafia bosses and Republican presidents in years to come.

For the Andersons, life became a struggle. Paul's mother, Elizabeth, went to work as a schoolteacher. Paul and his two sisters also went to work.

I don't know what Paul Anderson's middle name was. They say he was named for an uncle, but when Paul was 13, that uncle declined to give him a job he wanted. The willful Anderson resented the man so keenly that he legally changed his middle name to Y and wouldn't talk about it.

Paul rode his bike through town and found work delivering newspapers and telegrams. He attended Central High but didn't graduate. He found work as a copyboy for the *Knoxville Journal & Tribune*, then edited by elderly Union Captain William Rule. (Anderson was probably aware that one of Rule's former copyboys had become publisher of the *New York Times*.) The young Anderson occasionally got to write real articles and, apparently, did a good job of it.

By 1911, at age 18, Anderson was a full-fledged reporter, one of the stars of the Gay Street daily, a teenager writing front-page stories. A colleague on the *Journal* talked Anderson into moving to St. Louis; by 1913, he was there, soon working for the nationally respected *Post-Dispatch*.

For more than 20 years, Anderson would remain a hard-nosed South Knoxville brawler, but in a national ring. He became a legend for guts, once getting himself jailed just to extract a confession from a drug dealer. In 1917 he gained nationwide exposure for his coverage of a race riot, which he reported from the scene—they say he hammered the story out on his battered portable, still wearing his bloodstained shirt. Anderson would be among the most brutally honest reporters on the scene of the biggest stories of his day: the Scopes monkey trial, the Leopold and Loeb murder case, Al Capone's abduction of Chicago—and the Teapot Dome scandal.

Known for an almost feral ability to smell a lie, Anderson got on that case early on and didn't loosen his grip until oil magnate Harry Sinclair and former U.S. Secretary of the Interior Albert Fall were in prison. It was that relentless series of articles that won Anderson the 1929 Pulitzer.

Through multiple death threats, vicious rows with editors, and three bad marriages, Anderson returned home to Knoxville for several days every summer from 1913 to 1938 to visit his mother. When he was here, he almost always found time for a few rounds of golf at Holston Hills Country Club. For a profane, irreverent newspaperman sometimes branded "Bolshevik" by his big-business enemies, Anderson had an unusual fondness for that rich man's game—and an almost foppish flair for grooming uncharacteristic of the stereotypical hard-boiled reporter. Even on vacation he wore a three-piece suit and cream-colored spats, with a stylish dapper mustache, his hair slicked and parted on a jaunty off-center angle.

In other ways, unfortunately, Anderson fit the reporter stereotype. The '30s were hard on Anderson, but not for the same reasons they were hard on most folks: Anderson was, in fact, one of the best-paid reporters in Washington. But as he passed the age when his father died, he grew disillusioned with himself and with the human race. He began drinking more heavily, filing stories late. In early '38, when the *Post-Dispatch* caught him in a lie, they fired him.

He was still respected enough to find other work, but he no longer had a heart for it. He was back here one last time, for his 45th birthday in

August 1938. Squinting grimly in the summer sun, he posed for a picture with his third wife, his mother, and his sister, in front of his mother's house at 710 Phillips Avenue, a wooden house still standing near the south bank of the river.

Back in Washington three months later, Anderson told his maid, "My usefulness is at an end and I am tired of living." Paul Y. Anderson, Pulitzer-winning reporter, swallowed a handful of sleeping pills.

Labor leader John L. Lewis and Senator George Norris spoke at Anderson's Washington funeral. His family brought him home to be buried beside his father, the ill-fated quarryman. At his burial at Island Home Baptist Church were flowers from President Roosevelt and Supreme Court Justice Hugo Black. On his unusual headstone was inscribed the number 30—the old-time reporter's symbol for the end of a story.

—4/10/97

On Broadway

Forty years ago this week, a retired shoe salesman named Cornelius was keeping a room at the Park Hotel downtown. The 77-year-old man was married to a woman in Missouri with whom he'd had three kids, but he hadn't seen any of them in quite a while. For almost three months, Cornelius had been staying here in Knoxville. He told somebody he was here to revisit the scenes of his childhood.

He apparently had a lot of revisiting to do. He'd been here frequently in recent years, back home after straying for half a century, staying with his sister Ella or at the stately old Whittle Springs Hotel. But his sister and he didn't always get along—and then they'd closed Whittle Springs. Cornelius settled for a room at the Park, a cheaper hotel on Walnut.

There were few reminders of Victorian Knoxville still around to revisit in 1957. When Cornelius Coffin Williams had last lived here, Knoxville was a booming city with an opera house and a racetrack and an iron works and a big brewery and 100 saloons—a progressive town with a reputation for innovation, good race relations, and dynamic business; it was one of the wholesaling centers of the South, ambitious to be even bigger than that.

But the Knoxville Cornelius returned to was a humbler, more chastened place, still smarting from being called the Ugliest City in America a few years ago. And Knoxville was now dry. Wine, liquor, and everything but weak beer was illegal. Knoxville was also more strictly segregated than it had been in the last century. In 1957 even newspaper obituaries were segregated, the "Colored" column added at the end.

Just before the first day of spring, as Knoxville busied itself preparing its dogwood trails, Cornelius took ill and checked himself into St. Mary's Hospital that Friday. Just after midnight the following Wednesday morning, he died. We read about it, a small item on page 14 of the *Journal*, with a photograph of an awkward old man in a suit and glasses, a black hat on his head. The *News-Sentinel* featured the news a little more prominently: Tennessee Williams' Father Dies During Illness Here.

If Cornelius Coffin Williams had died a few decades earlier, headlines would have identified him by his relationship to his prominent attorney father, not his son. The Williams family was once among Knoxville's proudest. A descendant of both James White and John Sevier, Cornelius was heir to a legacy, a prince in any other era. But in 1957 the Williamses were nearly forgotten. Reporters for both papers got mixed up about the Williams ancestry, the legacy Cornelius apparently didn't inherit. No statesman or colonel, Cornelius Coffin Williams had spent his life selling shoes, drinking, and misunderstanding people. He might have admitted he hadn't been much of a father.

Cornelius had named one of his children Thomas Lanier Williams III, after his noble Knoxville forebears. But by 1957 his middle child was much better known as *Tennessee* Williams, the author of *The Glass Menagerie* and *A Streetcar Named Desire*. Even Knoxvillians who weren't literary sorts knew the name; several big Broadway hits and big motion pictures, always with big stars. Cornelius had gone to see one movie in Knoxville, the dark, sexually suspenseful *Baby Doll*. "I think it's a very fine picture and I'm proud of my son," he'd told a reporter afterward.

Tennessee Williams had just turned 46 when he was called to Knoxville. Cornelius's funeral was downtown at Mann's, with Jack McKinnon, the longtime minister of First Presbyterian, presiding. Williams recalled it in an essay called "The Man in the Overstuffed Chair," a bitter memoir about the father he tried to understand.

"The funeral was an exceptionally beautiful service," he recalled. "My brother, Aunt Ella, and I sat in a small room set apart for the nearest of kin and listened and looked on while the service was performed." Sister Rose, institutionalized, didn't make it.

"Then we went out to 'Old Gray,' as they called the Knoxville Cemetery, and there we sat in a sort of tent with the front of it open, to witness the interment of the man in the overstuffed chair."

He wrote that account soon after the funeral but chose not to publish it until 1980, near the end of his life. It now serves as the preface for his *Collected Stories.*

"I suspect, now, that he knew that I was more of a Williams than a Dakin," he wrote, comparing his parents' families, "and that I would be more and more like him as I grew older, and that he pitied me for it. I often wonder many things about my father now, and understand things about him, such as his anger at life, so much like my own...."

The essay also discloses what little he knew about his father's late-life companion, a widow from Toledo with whom elderly Cornelius kept company in Knoxville.

"Behind us, on chairs in the open, was a very large congregation of more distant kinfolk and surviving friends of his youth, and somewhere among them was the Toledo Widow, I've heard....The widow drove off in his car which he had bequeathed to her, her only bequest, and I've heard of her nothing more."

After the ceremony Williams caused a minor scandal when, in his white linen suit and sunglasses, the Broadway star sat on a nearby stone to sign autographs. (On a recent visit to Knoxville, a Tennessee Williams scholar remarked that if it's rude to sign autographs at your dad's funeral, maybe it's also rude to ask.)

After a few days in Knoxville, talking with Aunt Ella and visiting old family shrines, like the old Colonel John Williams house on Dandridge, Williams returned to New York, went into therapy, and wrote a terrifying family play called *Suddenly Last Summer.*

There at Old Gray, Cornelius Williams is buried alongside his parents and grandparents, but far from his wife and children—a simple stone by Old Gray's extravagant standards, just a few steps from Broadway.

—3/27/97

Liking It Better

How I came to be in his cabin in Norris that day had a lot to do with my friend Ron King, who came up with this idea to celebrate the bicentennial of the Bill of Rights. We'd consider the Constitution's first 10 amendments, finding an incident in Knoxville history that illustrated each. Then we'd get somebody to read it for a TV spot, some distinguished voice to tell the stories we'd written—illustrated, Ken Burns-style, with historical pictures.

The project didn't pay and had nothing to do with my full-time job editing a waiting-room magazine at Whittle, but scavenger hunts have always appealed to me, especially where Knoxville history is concerned. I don't even remember what we found. I wrote a few, Ron and another colleague wrote a few. We had 10 scripts telling 10 stories about the 10 rights. We just needed someone with a good voice to read them for us, on tape.

None of us knew Alex Haley, the Pulitzer-winner, Malcolm X's ghost-writer, inspiration behind the most popular TV mini-series in American history. But Ron contacted him somehow and asked him whether he'd even consider this volunteer project.

Come on up, Haley said. Sunday morning at 11:00, Ron and I and radio journalist Jean Ash, who had a big radio-quality tape recorder, drove up to Norris in Ron's truck and arrived at Alex Haley's farm.

The young guard at the gate let us pass. The compound looked like a rustic resort, cabins around a pond where white swans were swimming, brightly painted harvesting tools that obviously hadn't been used lately.

We walked across the famous porch. I'd heard John Rice Irwin talk about this porch, the only place he'd ever seen Alex Haley, Lamar Alexander, and Grandpa Jones at the same time. We walked inside, enveloped in the smell of green beans simmering in pork.

Three young women with Caribbean hair were just leaving. I figured we were penciled in from 11:00 to 11:15, 11:30 if we were lucky. The cook gave us some coffee, and we sat down, double-checking things, nervous about our scripts and what a famous author would think of them.

The front door opened, and suddenly there he was in the room with us: a short and, I couldn't help noticing, odd-looking man. His skin seemed distended, overinflated, buoyant. Something about him and the slow, gentle way he moved around reminded me of Winnie the Pooh. Still, he was businesslike as we shook hands, wanted to get right to work. I started to think we'd be out of there in 15 minutes, home by lunchtime. He wanted to read our scripts.

Ron had printed his stuff out on an old dot-matrix printer. "I hope you don't mind," he said.

"It's my favorite," Haley said. He wasn't smiling, but he wasn't exactly sarcastic. I didn't understand, at first, his backwards way of talking, his habit of saying the opposite of what he meant, in tones too even to sound facetious. (He asked whether the gatekeeper had given us any trouble and said he worried about the boy's "delicate feet"—then he mentioned that the kid wore a size-13 shoe.)

He sat there and read these scripts we'd been working on for several weeks, and said, mm-hm. Mm-hm. Then he got up and without comment disappeared into some other part of the house. Somebody said he'd gone to eat lunch.

We could wait, I figured. When Gertie the cook offered us lunch, I pictured some white-bread sandwiches. I said nothing for me, thanks. But I didn't understand. She conducted us into a sunny dining room where a table was laid with five settings of crystal and silver and plates of country ham, greens, sweet potatoes. George, the old man who'd come in with Haley, was already sitting at one end and, I recall, already eating. I stood there a minute before I realized this elegant table was set for us. We sat down and sipped on some very sweet iced tea. George wasn't in a mood to talk to strangers and didn't volunteer much.

We had just started eating the delicious meal when Alex Haley came in and sat at the head of the table just to my right. Someone passed him the ham, and he said, "I don't care much for this" and served himself a few thick slices.

He didn't seem especially interested in us and didn't expect us to be especially interested in him, either. Still, it was comfortable somehow, one of the most pleasant meals I've had in years. It reminded me of the silent lunches I once ate with my grandfather—*dinner*, he always called it—after we'd been out working in the yard all morning. I felt like a kid.

When Haley asked me to pass the ham, I was careful not to drop it.

But, like my grandfather, if you asked him questions, he'd usually answer them. Ron asked him why he liked to write on freighters. "Because you don't have to listen to 800 people dancing on the deck above you," he said.

I'd always wondered why Haley, raised in West Tennessee, where *Roots* is set, where Chicken George is buried, chose to settle here. Only because I thought I would regret it later if I didn't, I asked.

"I like East Tennessee better," he said. I waited for him to elaborate, but he did not. He was beginning to seem more like Buddha than Pooh.

Ron asked him what he was working on now. He mentioned the *Queen* project, said they were casting it for a TV miniseries. It concerned a young mulatto woman, he said, and asked us if we knew any good mulatto actresses. He stopped eating and looked at me, as if expecting I might name the star of his next TV series. I thought desperately but couldn't come up with any names at all, probably couldn't recall my own without stuttering.

Then he said he was at work on an even bigger project, a novel about a white Appalachian family. "It should explode a lot of stereotypes," he said. Then he added, as if we might be skeptical, "It's an *excellent* book."

During the meal, large flats materialized, page proofs from *Parade* magazine, an essay Haley had written for the 50th anniversary of the bombing of Pearl Harbor, and he went over them as we had dessert.

It wasn't until after the leisurely dinner that we got around to the project at hand. We took care of that relatively quickly, in another room of the house. Patiently he read our scripts into the microphone, redoing a few when he didn't get a name just right.

He seemed tired by it, and relieved it was over. More relaxed, he showed us around. He was especially proud of an antique organ he showed us, and an old pharmacist's desk, and a grandfather clock. But I couldn't help noticing that neither in here nor in the big common room, nor anywhere else I could see in this main house, were any books at all, not his, not anybody's. I was told this wasn't the house he lived in, he just did his entertaining here. Still, I wondered. You can spot *Roots* in the background bookshelves in any number of *Southern Living* model dens. Most people decorate with books, even if they don't actually read them.

Alex Haley, author of one of America's all-time best-sellers, did not.

We'd been his guests for three or four hours. Before we left, I mentioned a magazine project I was working on at Whittle. Inspired by a scene in a Woody Allen movie, it was a short serial feature called "What Makes Life Worth Living." We got celebrities to give us their ideas, lists of favorite dishes, pieces of music, meteorological phenomena. Haley seemed interested. Send him a letter, he said, grinning, and then "let my guilt work on me."

I left convinced I'd hear from him, and flattered myself with the notion that Alex Haley and I might get to be pals, that we might hang out down at Lucille's and talk about the Coast Guard, Malcolm X, jazz in the '40s.

I sent him that letter and was waiting to hear from him about what makes life worth living when, not three months later, I heard Alex Haley had died.

The worst of the attacks on his reputation as an author and as an honest man followed in short order and continue today. That huge new bronze statue of him looking south from that hillside in Morningside Park looks exactly as I remember him, just as comfortable and just as mysterious as he seemed seated at the head of his dinner table in 1991. I can't say I got to know Alex Haley, and I can't vouch for the way he chose to write a book. But the man who's there on our hillside forever looks honest to me.

—*4/23/98*

CHAPTER FOUR

TOUGH GUYS

Easy, Gentlemen!

It's early evening in Knoxville, the first chilly day of the fall. "The nights are pinching cool now," as they said in 1871, down in the 40s. People were still talking about last weekend's circus, the "Wild Tartarian Monster Yak," and Old Emperor, the "War Elephant," who paraded down Gay Street Saturday. But now farmers were preparing for Fair season opening next week, harvest-time exhibits along with some big-money horse races. Downtown, sentimentalists were looking forward to the smells of the sidewalk chestnut vendors who'd surely be here soon.

That Wednesday Perez Dickinson's store had a fresh shipment of black alpaca. A few blocks down, the Great New York Grocery advertised English Breakfast tea, "Old Governor" Java Coffee, dried herring, New York cheese, Havana Cigars.

At sunset the full moon was hardly visible in a hazy sky. On Gay Street a group of men, weary of discussing business, were ambling toward the St. Nicholas Saloon for a drink. The well-known establishment at the base of a hotel at Gay and Main was the chief competition for its nearest neighbor, the Lamar House, just across Cumberland. The St. Nick was known for its fresh beer and Norfolk oysters.

The men might have seen the saloon's ad in that afternoon's *Daily*

Press & Herald: Playfully exaggerating local enthusiasm for their oysters, the St. Nicholas ad warned, *Take it easy, gentlemen! Take it easy!*

One of those gentlemen outside the St. Nicholas was 44-year-old General J.H. Clanton, of Montgomery, Alabama. General Clanton was a revered veteran of Shiloh and a Democratic politician, here representing his home state in a railroad controversy.

The stocky general in a gray cashmere suit was conversing with prominent Knoxvillian A.S. Prosser when one Tomlinson Fort, an adversary in the railroad case, introduced Clanton to a 26-year-old Union veteran, Colonel Dave Nelson. Nelson was the son of Tennessee Supreme Court Justice T.A.R. Nelson, who'd been one of President Johnson's attorneys during the late impeachment trial. Dave Nelson, an attorney himself and sometime Republican politician, seemed a promising legacy. But that Wednesday, young Colonel Nelson had been drinking.

Perhaps naively, Mr. Fort—a former Confederate officer himself—introduced Nelson as a man who had "fought us" six years ago. From that first handshake, Nelson and Clanton didn't hit it off. The men were strolling in the direction of the St. Nicholas when Nelson, hands in pockets, began speaking elliptically about "a certain place in the city" that he would show General Clanton—"if he was not afraid to go."

Colonel Nelson should have known that wasn't something you'd say to a veteran of Shiloh, especially one from Alabama. His hands clutching his cashmere lapels, General Clanton stopped and demanded to know what the younger man meant by the remark. If Nelson thought the General was afraid of anything, Clanton said, he might as well "pick his ground and settle it then and there." The shouting got the attention of a customer in Room 10 of the Lamar House, who watched the proceedings from his window. Nelson was especially agitated. "Keep cool, Dave," Fort said, without effect.

Panicked by this burly Alabama Confederate who'd just challenged him to a duel, Nelson ran ahead into the saloon, re-emerging with a double-barrel shotgun. Partly shielded by a beer barrel, he steadied his gun against an awning support.

Clanton asked Tomlinson to pace them apart for a proper duel. Tomlinson declined, estimating that Nelson was too drunk to duel. Clanton stood his ground. Nelson fired. Clanton drew a pistol and fired.

Clanton was still standing with his pistol raised when Nelson fired his second barrel, and hit. Clanton crumpled slowly forward on the pavement. The first to reach him was a black boy, perhaps a servant. "Take my hat and pistol," Clanton told him. "I have done all I can."

Nelson fled again inside the St. Nicholas Saloon, escaping through the back door. He made his way to his dad's home on Cumberland, confessed to his father that he'd shot a man, and then slipped away. He left on a borrowed horse, riding west just past sunset.

Clanton's friends carried his bleeding body into a confectionary at the Lamar House. It was the same building where, not eight years earlier, another young wounded general, named Sanders, had been brought to die. They counted 20 wounds in Clanton's right side, at least 15 of which had pierced his chest, severing arteries, and piercing a lung.

General Clanton's corpse lay in state at the Lamar House library, available for public viewing.

A block away mortician L.C. Shepherd advertised that with the help of Taylor's Patent Corpse Preserver, "I am prepared to keep bodies from four to six days before putting them into coffins, when desired." Clanton's party didn't bother. They carried his body straight down Gay to the train station for the midnight train to Alabama. An impromptu inquest that night at the Lamar House considered the murder of General Clanton.

Meanwhile, Sheriff Gossett pursued Nelson well into the chilly night, out Kingston Pike. He encountered several witnesses along the way, including an ailing liveryman who apparently knew Nelson—but was so agitated upon learning he'd helped a murderer flee that moments after talking to the sheriff, he died, too. Nelson was last spotted several miles to the southwest, apparently on his way home to Cleveland. At some point, he was likely passed by the train bearing General Clanton's corpse.

Nelson reappeared in Knoxville two days later and turned himself in, pleading not guilty: he said he'd shot Clanton in self-defense. His famous father quit the state Supreme Court to help. After two years of delays, the trial focused on Clanton's alleged violent nature. After deliberating, the jury read its surprise verdict: *not guilty*.

The whole state of Alabama screamed foul. Some declared the shooting was a political assassination and that Knoxville's justice system was implicated. General Clanton became an Alabama martyr.

Today Clanton, Alabama, is a thriving town of 8,000 on the road from Montgomery to Birmingham.

—9/26/96

Naked and Uncovered

A town's vital statistics are often just conclusions waiting to be jumped to. Mid-1800s Knoxville had a population of only a couple thousand. Combine that figure with a bucolic location, and you start to come up with phrases like "sleepy little town," a cliché historians have often used to describe pre-Civil War Knoxville.

But was Knoxville ever a "sleepy little town"? Maybe for a spell in the mid-1840s, I once figured, after we'd lost State Capital status, after our experiments in publishing books about incest and serial killers fizzled, after the heyday of the downtown distilling industry, after we'd filled in the Church Street cock-fighting pit, after the corpse-shocking fad was over...but just *before* the arrival of the wine-making, love-feasting Swiss immigrants; the railroad-building, saloon-keeping Irish; and piano-playing, beer-brewing Germans; and just before the arrival of Parson Brownlow and his *Whig*, printed each week in pure black venom.

All that commenced in the *late* 1840s. Maybe, excepting the presence of popular blasphemer/humorist George Harris, Knoxville was arguably a "sleepy little town" for about three years in the mid-1840s.

I used to say that, anyway—until I learned that this Monday is the Sesquicentennial of the Exposure of Kingsberry York.

A century and a half ago, an advertiser in the Knoxville *Register* was railing against "the would-be Knoxville aristocracy," alleging that "there are *villains* here, as *base* as can be found in any other town or country."

He didn't name names, but 1846 clearly wasn't Knoxville's finest hour. After years of trying, we were still stranded with no railroad; nobody'd succeeded in laying tracks through the mountains. Some so-called cities with silly names like "Atlanta," places that didn't even exist when Knoxville was a capital, were suddenly booming, just because they had a few dang railroad tracks.

Some were giving up on this weird little valley town with clay streets and a swamp that stank in hot weather and still no city-style gaslights. Stores closed, others consolidated. Both local hotels were for rent to any proprietor who dared take them on.

But in downtown bookstores you could buy the works of Byron, Scott, Cervantes, and Cicero, along with treatises on Hebrew grammar, astronomy, animal magnetism, manure. And at the wharf Deery and Company unloaded exotic cargo from the riverboat *Enterprise*—Baltimore Rio Coffee, Gunpowder Tea, tropical figs, La India cigars, chocolate, blasting powder—all for sale at Deery's riverfront store. If you didn't have money, they'd take trade: beeswax, feathers, ginseng.

Some things were looking up. It wasn't paid for yet, but the new School for the Deaf was rising on the hillside northwest of town. The tiny university, sequestered on its hilltop, anticipated the winter session, opening the 15th. (Its few dozen students wore democratic drab; expensive fabrics and fancy shoes were strictly banned.)

If we didn't have railroads or gaslights, we did have a newer, more amazing technology: photography. Daguerrotypist T.H. Smiley was in town, "taking likenesses of those who may desire it…equal to the best taken in any of the eastern cities."

We don't know whether Mr. Smiley got a chance to get a likeness of Mr. York, or desired it.

Knoxville's once-strong Temperance movement, some feared, was dead. The Knoxville Drug Store, on Gay, sold lots of stuff—lemon syrup, palm soap, Persian scent bags, Scotch snuff. Judging by the emphasis in their ads, though, they were proudest of one staple product: OPIUM. "Cheap and genuine drugs for cash" was their motto. Maybe that's what made us so sleepy.

We don't know whether Mr. York was a customer. All we know about the noble Kingsberry York, and it's not much, is from the circuit court dockets—which tell the tale of a singular incident downtown on Wednesday, October 14.

"Kingsberry York, late of Knox County," duly recorded the sleepytown court clerk, "in the presence of divers citizens…as well men as women…passing and re-passing…unlawfully, wickedly, and scandalously did expose to the view of said persons so present…the privy parts and organs of generation of him, the said Kingsberry York, naked and uncovered for a long space of time, to wit, for a span of 15 minutes...."

The attorney general added that York's adventure contributed "to the manifest corruption of the public morals" and was an "evil example to all like offenders," a "nuisance of all persons passing and re-passing."

Whether Mr. York was a common exhibitionist, a maverick nudist, an oblivious addict, or a careless drunk, we don't know. But it's fair to say that for at least 15 minutes in 1846, Knoxville was wide awake.

—10/10/96

The Exchange of Worlds

A few months ago a couple of readers showed me an article called "Blind Justice," by Arkansas scholar Daniel Sutherland, in *Civil War Times*. I'd missed it. Most of the magazines I find time to read these days are the tahini-stained ones on the rack at the Tomato Head. I've only rarely spotted *Civil War Times* there. Anyway, these folks passed along this vivid story I'd never heard, about a Confederate horseman of the legendary Texas Rangers who inadvertently found himself in a cold place called Knoxville, a city he should have been nowhere near, 133 years ago this Christmas. This rebel in a Mexican serape was here awaiting court martial on charges of espionage.

You never know with spies. During the Civil War many people said they weren't spies, of course, but actually were. Some even claimed they were spies but actually weren't. One of the last Confederate spies who'd visited was the famous Belle Boyd, sent here by Stonewall Jackson for her own safety. Only a few months ago, she'd been welcomed to Confederate-dominated Knoxville with a pageant that must have been embarrassing for any spy: speeches, a brass band, enthusiastic ovations. The local Confederate families feted *La Belle Rebelle* at local ballrooms for weeks.

It was an unrecognizably different Knoxville that Ephraim Dodd entered later the same year. The soldiers patrolling Gay Street were now dressed in blue. They'd just repelled a frontal assault by Confederates attempting to regain the city they'd carelessly lost two months ago.

Dodd was a 24-year-old Kentucky native known for his "uniform," which was flamboyant even for a Texas Ranger: a captured Yankee overcoat, unmatched blue pants, a broad-brimmed Ranger hat decorated with a Texas star, and a colorful Mexican serape. When he arrived here on December 18, Dodd was accompanied by two Rebel colleagues and a Union military guard. When they were locked in the Knox County Jail on Hill Avenue, they were only POWs, unfortunate stragglers from Longstreet's fleeing Confederate force, an abortive horse-requisition party who'd spent the last five cold days running through Loudon, Blount, and Sevier counties, trying to sneak around Knoxville to safety. But Sevier County, allegedly the most pro-Union county in the entire country, south *and* north, was the wrong place for Confederates to hide. Loyal citizens tipped off the Home Guards, who collared Dodd and his cronies and took them into Knoxville, where Burnside's well-fortified Union army now presided.

One of the three gave in and swore loyalty to the Union. Dodd did not. He sent a letter to the local Masonic lodge; some of the brethren tried but couldn't help. Meanwhile, the prisoners were, Dodd wrote, "freezing and starving by inches." Christmas Day came and went. Dodd and his fellow prisoners actually looked forward to an anticipated transfer to a Northern prison camp.

Sometime late in December, the Union captors paid closer attention to this Confederate's odd attire—especially that Union coat and blue pants. It wasn't all that unusual for Confederate soldiers to wear whatever clothes were at hand, even Union coats, especially in cold weather. But one who'd been using the blue to pass himself off as a Union soldier was something else altogether.

Dodd's most damning accessory, though, wasn't his coat or his pants or his Mexican serape, but a diary. In Loudon County, he'd noted in his pocket journal during his trek, pro-Union citizens didn't harass him because they thought he was a Union soldier. Those passages were read aloud before strangers in his Knoxville court martial, probably on New Year's Day, 1864. On the strength of the diary, the court martial convicted Dodd of spying, the sentence for which was well known.

Rev. Joseph Martin, from Second Presbyterian, prayed with Dodd. Confederate sympathizers filed late-night motions with federal authorities, who ignored them. Dodd learned about his sentence only two days before his already-scheduled hanging. He took some of his few remaining moments to write a letter to his parents in Kentucky. "Under very different circumstances from those by which I was surrounded when I last wrote you, I write this letter," he opened. "I am under close guard, and under sentence of death…" He denied the allegations, said they didn't even hold up in court; but that he was condemned anyway.

"I am treated as kindly by the guard as could be expected," he continued. "The Rev. Mr. Martin, of the Presbyterian Church, is visiting me and affording me much consolation. I feel, dear father and mother, that if I suffer the penalty tomorrow, the exchange of worlds will be for the better…Do not grieve, dear parents, for I am leaving a world of sin and misery for one of perfect bliss. I can say no more…."

Snow was on the ground that Friday morning as Rev. Martin escorted Dodd from his cell. Dodd climbed onto a wagon already loaded with an empty coffin. Wearing his sombrero and Mexican serape, his eyes cast down at nothing in particular, Dodd rode there on his own long box, between rows of slowly marching blue-suited soldiers in a grim parade up Gay Street, as the fife-and-drum corps played the Death March. They say even Union soldiers teared up.

At the north end of Gay, near the train station, Dodd mounted the waiting gallows and told a soldier, "I die innocent of the charge against me." At 11:00, the door opened, and Dodd fell—all the way to the ground. The rope had broken. Soldiers waited for the semi-conscious Dodd to revive—apparently it was against regulations to hang an unconscious man—and then they hanged him again, this time with a double noose. By 11:30 Ephraim Dodd was dead. They fired a big gun to announce the army surgeon's diagnosis.

The news brought national outrage, even up North. Dodd was reportedly buried somewhere in Knoxville, probably in Old Gray, under a headboard. I've looked for Ephraim Dodd's grave but haven't found it.

—*12/19/96*

The Battle of Depot Street

People don't talk much about Depot Street. Across the tracks from the Old City, it's just north of what most folks think of as Downtown. Still, it's home to several interesting businesses. On its east end, for example, are East Tennessee's only bottling brewery and East Tennessee's only opera company. Near Gay Street are the old Southern station and Knoxville's best-known and (arguably) oldest restaurant.

But Regas prefers to say they're on North Gay. You may never have heard of Depot Street, even if you've been on it a hundred times. Even as businesses thrive here, the street itself keeps a low profile. The couple of blocks to the west of Gay, where Depot takes an odd 45-degree turn to intersect Broadway, are the quietest.

On a late-winter Monday morning, you might walk down the middle of West Depot and not worry too much about encountering anybody at all, either on foot or driving a car. But on another Monday morning one century ago, 2,000 Knoxville men, black and white, were fighting for the right to be here. Some had shovels, some had firehoses, some had guns, some had warrants. It was this little bent elbow of Depot for which Knoxville's best and brightest risked their reputations as reasonable men, and for which one gave his life.

This business had started almost eight years before, when a green kid named William Gibbs McAdoo mortgaged his future to buy Knoxville's mule-drawn streetcar system. Then only 25, McAdoo was a successful attorney who'd already been president of a couple of small businesses. He'd grown up in Knoxville, the son of impractically intellectual parents who taught history and wrote poetry. Like many professors' kids, McAdoo was frustrated with his parents' sacrifices and was determined to do something more practical with his own life. He dropped out of UT but passed the bar anyway and found work in Chattanooga.

McAdoo returned home with a business idea so ambitious and unusual that conservative Knoxville investors weren't much interested in risking money on it. Undaunted, McAdoo went to New York and found a spectral investor named J. Simpson Africa. McAdoo returned with the capital and in 1889 went to work. He bought Knoxville's mule-drawn trolley system, expanded it—and *electrified it.* Here McAdoo built one of the South's first electric transportation systems.

McAdoo's Knoxville Street Railway opened in 1890 with a grand electric trip down Magnolia to Chilhowee Park, and great hurrahs for the kid with the big idea.

But McAdoo's equipment wasn't up to the strain of modern electrical industry. The line broke down even more often than the mules had.

Within two years his electric streetcar line was bankrupt. William Gibbs McAdoo wasn't even 30 yet, but already he'd suffered a business loss so massive it would have impressed the Butchers.

Desperate for income, he set himself up as an attorney in New York, moving his young family into an apartment on 87th—while back in Knoxville a hard-nosed Ohio opportunist named C.C. Howell took over McAdoo's electric streetcar system and somehow made it work. McAdoo rankled at the idea of a Yankee interloper taking his place in his home-town. McAdoo was rising in New York law and politics, but in 1896 he was back here, trying to defend his turf and redeem his fiasco.

Though business competition is sometimes described as "cutthroat," it rarely results in actual combat. One century ago, it did.

McAdoo bought part of his old streetcar route, including the steam "dummy" route to Fountain City, and began building new tracks to form a rival company, democratically known as the Citizens Street Railway. Howell made it as difficult for him as possible, thwarting McAdoo's access to his old rail lines, especially at crucial Depot Street, which linked Broadway to the Southern terminal.

McAdoo's work crew of 200 men, previously unemployed laborers who were grateful for the work, arrived at Depot Street before dawn with wag-onloads of shovels and picks; by 5:30 a.m., they were tearing up the city streets. Howell's associates heard the noise and called the cops. Three Knoxville policemen arrived and began charging the crew with violating an obscure ordinance about digging up city streets during the cooler months. Theoretically, all 200 laborers were under arrest. But they outnumbered the police and ignored their status. A few were hauled away, but most of the laborers kept working as black gandy dancers sang work songs.

Meanwhile, still before working hours, McAdoo's men approached a judge, who found reason to believe they might have some right to tear up Depot Street and that it was inappropriate to arrest them for doing so. With a warrant in hand, Knox County deputies arrived at Depot to arrest Knoxville Police for arresting honest laborers.

It went back and forth like that as the sun came up, and the crowd of laborers and spectators grew larger and more frenzied, now more than 1,000, an estimated 800 of whom were sympathetic with McAdoo's 200.

By 7:00 a.m., a wagon with railroad ties arrived; the police chief himself was on the scene and failed to halt the work by arresting the foreman. Frustrated police rang the rarely heard Riot Alarm: four rings from the bell on Market Square, and every policeman in town was called to quell the riot. When a platoon of helmeted policemen arrived, however, there were plenty of sheriff's deputies to arrest them, too. At one time, even the police chief and the mayor were, theoretically, under arrest.

Finally the fire department took them all by surprise, setting up hoses at either end of Depot, opening the spigots, and, without warning, clearing crowded Depot Street with twin blasts of city water.

"Frantic men, angry laborers, vociferous sympathizers, innocent onlookers, and helpless women and children all made a wild rush…to escape the bath that was about to be enforced on them."

The frustrated laborers, many of whom hadn't worked in months, attacked the firemen with bricks. One black worker attempted to cut the offending firehose with a knife. As the fire chief attempted to prevent him, one of the older workers, a black man named Will Arnold, attacked the fire chief with a pick handle, knocking him senseless. Arnold then swung at a policeman, who shot him twice.

As Arnold lay dying, the huge crowd began shouting "Cold-Blooded Murder!", "Hang the Police!", and "Hurrah for McAdoo!" Several others were injured in what the *New York Times* headlined SMALL RIOT IN KNOXVILLE.

Sam Heiskell, the young first-term mayor of Knoxville facing his first major crisis, appeared, appealing for calm. He climbed up on a fence at that bend in Depot Street and pleaded, "In behalf of law and order, I ask and appeal to you to disperse. Go to your homes and let this matter be settled in the courts!" The mob hooted Mayor Heiskell off his fence; the contractor told his men to go back to work. McAdoo himself was there, proudly surveying his intrepid warrior-laborers' incredible progress in laying a railway in what had, a few hours ago, been an intact city street. The young attorney stepped up onto a stone wall across Depot from where the Mayor had spoken. "We have commenced this work," McAdoo declared, "and propose to continue it until it is finished!" The crowd cheered.

Wagons carrying the rails arrived to fix to the ties already in place.

Sheriff Groner spoke, declaring he'd arrest anyone who interfered—"it matters not who he might be." The embarrassed mayor and police chief couldn't have missed the hint; both were already under arrest. But at the courthouse, Mayor/suspect Heiskell obtained an injunction from another judge to stop work, one the sheriff apparently couldn't argue with. At 10:30 a.m., the workers finally laid down their tools.

In his first of many trials by fire, Mayor Heiskell eventually prevailed. In a lawsuit McAdoo eventually lost control of Knoxville's streetcar systems, both the first one he'd started and the second one he intended to compete with it. Both of McAdoo's lines were consolidated under Howell's guidance. As a legacy of capitalism at its most warlike, turn-of-the-century Knoxville had inherited one of the South's finest public-transit systems.

McAdoo returned to New York and his thriving career in politics. Four years after the Battle of Depot Street, McAdoo headed up the effort to build the first subway tunnel under New York's Hudson River, apparently without inciting any riots. Twenty years after he was arrested in downtown Knoxville, William Gibbs McAdoo was U.S. secretary of the treasury—and as co-founder of the Federal Reserve System, one of the most influential men ever to occupy that office. Later still, McAdoo was U.S. senator from California—and three times a strong contender for the presidency. Despite historians' assessments that McAdoo was better fit to be president than most actual presidents are, he came close but never quite grasped the Democratic nomination.

McAdoo's memoirs, *Crowded Years*, are remarkably forthright about many of his failings but mention nothing about the Battle of Depot Street and the man who died for the streetcar track that was never finished. McAdoo did describe the failure of his original electric streetcar line, however—and suggested that the magnitude of his failure in Knoxville made unusual success on a national scale not only desirable, but necessary.

—2/27/97

Strange Distinctiveness:
The Disappointed Odyssey of the
S.S. *Oliver King*

For the next few years, people will argue about whether the new century officially begins in 2000 or 2001. The computer chaos promised when millions of circuits switch from 99 to 00 may settle the issue for us moderns, but it was an issue Knoxvillians argued about in 1899.

Hosting a formal "20th Century Day," the educated ladies of the Ossoli Circle threw down their gauntlet, declaring the 20th century did properly begin on Jan. 1, 1900. The editors of both the *Journal* and the *Sentinel,* however, steadfastly insisted the 20th century wouldn't be here until 1901. "Those who insist that today is the beginning of a new century can have it that way if they want to," allowed the *Journal.* "But they will find themselves out of line."

Still, the *Sentinel* used the occasion to speculate about the wonders of the century to come. "The 20th century will probably witness the end of war. It will see all the barbarous races of the world civilized....It may see all current languages reduced to two—Russian and English....Every village in the world will be in instantaneous telephonic communication with every other. The powers of the wind, the sun, and the sea will be chained, so that the air will no longer be fouled with smoke....The men of the 20th century will...solve the social problem....They will secure that fair relation between services and earnings for which the transitional 19th century has been vainly striving...."

As it turned out, there was a lot of vain striving in those last days of 1899. With sub-freezing weather for days, the Pigeon River froze, stranding the Knoxville riverboat *Flora Swan.* Even the Tennessee was icing over at its shallower spots, especially the half-mile strip along the south bank, downriver from the new Gay Street Bridge. It happened so often that the smart downtown hardware merchants kept a supply of ice skates on hand. At that one patch alone, someone counted 350 skaters. "The white ice was dotted with men and boys in black, darting here and there like so many miller bugs in a millpond," reported the *Journal.* "Here and there were some who...whirled, twisted, and flung their legs and bodies about, leaving behind them markings as odd as Egyptian hieroglyphics...."

A club of local sportsmen might have done well to study those hieroglyphics. Apparently confident of the liquid state of the Tennessee one Friday evening, these men, "a gang of the gambling fraternity," commandeered the well-known steamboat *Oliver King* at the Market Street wharf. They "slipped aboard with coops of poultry"—fancy gamecocks, to be specific. These sportsmen were taking their pets on a voyage to a quiet arena several miles downriver, to an island in the river near the Loudon county line, where there was a cave: "an ideal place for such affairs."

There in the cave, on this secluded island, they'd stage a championship cockfight, a big-money entertainment already illegal in Knoxville. They had every good intention of returning the riverboat to its wharf before dawn after their subterranean bird-bludgeoning tournament.

Five miles down the river that night, our sportsmen may have been arguing about what century it would soon be when, in the vicinity of Lyons Bend, the *Oliver King* bottomed out on a sandbar. Ice floes gathered around the ship, and despite the amateur rivermen's efforts, the *King* held fast. They watched the surface of the river freeze around them.

"There they struck," wrote the *Journal's* laconic reporter after it was all over, "and there they were stuck....There was dire distress with no lighthouse or rescue station in sight." In those days few lived along the river in west Knox County. No one could hear them scream.

"The steamboat sounded a weird note of distress," reported the *Journal*, "but the only answer was a mocking echo from the hills." They were still there when "the gamecocks aboard announced the dawn of day."

The mariners settled in for the weekend. "Saturday was an uneventful day, as the logbook of the vessel will show," wrote the mercilessly wry *Journal* correspondent. "Sunday dawned and wore on. The passengers aboard had by this time reached a famishing stage and a consultation was held as to whether the cork life-preservers should be eaten...." Apparently the sportsmen's well-bred pets weren't on the table.

Of all the Knoxville scenes of that colorful era, this one is my very favorite: this delegation of sportsmen contemplating cork rings aboard a highjacked steamboat loaded with crates of angry chickens in the middle of a half-frozen river. I wish Currier and Ives had been alive to print one last romantic river lithograph: *A Winter's Day Aboard the Oliver King*.

Sunday the temperature was down to nine degrees. But sometime that afternoon, a daredevil's yawl appeared on the water's surface, plowed through the ice, and came to the sportsmen's aid. Only he didn't have room in his boat for any chickens.

The weekend pirates abandoned ship and their colorful gamecocks and disembarked on the north shore, apparently along Lyons Bend—where some alarmed neighbors mistook them for "escaped inmates of the insane asylum." From a house they telephoned for horse-drawn cabs to come pick them up.

These daring mariners apparently tried to keep their river odyssey quiet. Frustrated reporters apologized that their story, as it stands, is all "that could be gathered from the participants, who were too disgusted to tell all particulars."

The night of their return, Knoxville celebrated that odd-looking new year, 1900—whatever century it might be. There were several drinking parties in town, called "watches," but Methodists went to church for a two-hour midnight prayer vigil. Bell-ringers showed up at nearly every church that had a bell tower. At midnight, according to the *Journal* account, "their musical clangor sounded with strange distinctiveness at that still hour. If it stirred the slumber of the sleeping city, it must have set it to pleasant dreaming."

—12/24/97

The Last Hanged Man

It was only March, and Sheriff Columbus Reeder was already hanging his third murderer of the year. Executions weren't rare in 1908 Knoxville, but some things made this one distinct. For one thing, the convict's defense attorney was John Houk, the former Republican congressman. He'd taken his client's case all the way to the state Supreme Court, to no avail.

Much more than his celebrity defense attorney, however, what made the condemned man especially different was that he was white. The men the Knox County sheriff routinely executed were black, many of them illiterate desperadoes who'd knifed somebody down in Cripple Creek or the Bowery. This man was, by contrast, a middle-class doctor's son. He'd gotten the death penalty because one of the two people he killed that summer night in 1906 had been a sheriff's deputy.

Sheriff Reeder was likely concerned about crowd control. The last time they'd hanged a white man in Knoxville was more than 30 years ago, and more than 20,000 came to watch. In a town hardly bigger than that crowd, it had caused problems. But this was a new century. Things were changing fast; Knoxville had proven itself a modern, progressive city by closing its 100 saloons just four months ago. Knoxville didn't have a working model of that new innovation, the electric chair, yet, but by recent state legislation, executions were now held behind the thick walls of the fortresslike jailhouse, inside, away from the crowd. The public execution was going the way of the saloon and other disorderly leftovers of the 19th century. Still, outside the jail, along Hill and Market Streets, crowds formed, hoping to catch a glimpse of something.

The management of Staub's Theater must have watched enviously. From the ticket window at Gay and Cumberland, they could see part of the crowd, back behind the courthouse. As it happened, that same Monday the large performance hall, built 35 years ago as an opera house, was taking a chance with a new idea: vaudeville matinees on weekdays. They'd booked a great lineup: comedians, high-wire stunts, cinematographic motion pictures—most of them short, comic black-and-white silents—plus a performance by Clarence Siegel, King of the Mandolin and Banjo. But it was not an auspicious day to launch a new afternoon entertainment in downtown Knoxville. If few showed up for the 3:30 show on that rainy Monday, it may have been due to the unexpected competition not three blocks away.

John McPherson's photograph had been in the papers. A fresh-faced, blue-eyed young man with his thick dark hair parted in the middle—in the photo he looked a little uncomfortable in his high Edwardian collar and tie. His picture didn't tell much of his story. Despite the esteem with which John McPherson spoke of his father, Dr. M.A. "Buck" McPherson had a criminal record himself. Convicted of murdering another physician back in '97—a dispute over a female patient, allegedly—Dr. McPherson had been released for good behavior and had somehow recovered his medical career. But he and his son apparently shared a taste for the demi-monde, the shadowy underworld of saloons and whorehouses along Florida Street, Knoxville's famous red-light district on the eastern edge of downtown. On July 14, 1906, they found themselves celebrating Bastille Day with a few drinks down there. Father and son were feeling pretty good at about 10:00 on that warm, damp night when they went up to the door of a well-known dance hall and brothel, the establishment of Nettie Hall, near Jackson Avenue. But Nettie disliked something about this pair in her parlor and refused them entrance to her dance hall. The younger McPherson, known for his "high-strung and nervous" temperament, drew his pistol and knocked the madame to the floor with the butt of his gun, accidentally firing it into the ceiling. When Nettie's husband, Grant Smith, appeared to help, McPherson shot him in the gut. It was said Dr. McPherson finished the man off with his scalpel.

The partiers hopped in their buggy and picked up Lizzie, John's live-in sweetheart, to seek refuge with relatives in Sevier County. They were six miles out of town on Sevierville Pike when they collided with a buggy driven by another physician on a late-night house call. Investigating the accident as the McPhersons tried to repair their axle, Knox County deputy William Walker recognized John and attempted to arrest the wanted man. McPherson shot him. For a week as McPherson made his way across county and then state lines, Deputy Walker lay dying. Nearly a year later they caught McPherson hiding in Radford, Virginia, and brought him back to face charges for the two murders. He was convicted in a two-week trial. Killing a deputy was a capital offense, even for a white man.

A lot of people saw something worthwhile about the troubled boy. John Houk organized a petition drive to save him from the death penalty, gathering thousands of signatures. He arranged a meeting between John's long-suffering mother and Governor Patterson; by March he was sure a pardon was on the way.

McPherson hardly slept the night before, rose early, and declined breakfast. He drank a cup of coffee as family and Baptist clergymen stood against the bars in the corridor of the Knox County jail, praying and singing hymns like "I'm Going Home to Die No More."

That afternoon it rained. They canceled the Central High baseball game at Chilhowee Park. Some 2,500 applied to get a seat to see the white man hang. But unlike those ugly spectacles of the 1800s, this was to be a modern, humane execution. It was to be private. The execution was scheduled for 2:00, but Houk convinced Sheriff Reeder a call from the governor was imminent. At 3:15, Reeder said he could wait no longer. The party left for the scaffold, singing "Other Refuge Have I None." Dr. William Atchley, pastor of the Broadway Baptist Church, read McPherson's statement: "I have very little to say. Talking will not better my condition." He went on to forgive "everybody who has wronged me," and to thank his family and lawyer. He asked forgiveness of "all whom I may have wronged." The sheriff asked McPherson if he had anything to add. McPherson himself spoke—"in a fine voice," they said later—insisting that his father had nothing to do with Deputy Walker's killing. Then he shook hands with everybody present: family, clergy, policemen, reaching down from the scaffold.

"Goodbye, Brother Atchley," he said to the minister.

"We'll meet beyond," Atchley said.

They fitted a black hood over his head, and Sheriff Reeder asked, "Are you ready, John?"

McPherson responded, "Wait a minute," and took a deep, clean breath. He didn't say he was ready to die.

The sheriff asked again. McPherson said only, "Goodbye. Goodbye. Goodbye…." Sheriff Reeder pulled the lever, and the trap door dropped. At 4:17 the medical examiner pronounced John McPherson dead.

Outside, stretching north almost to Main Street, east toward Gay Street, west toward Walnut, was a "great sea of umbrellas." They were 3,000 Knoxvillians, mostly white. None had witnessed any part of the hanging, but they seemed hushed, "curious but not demonstrative," unaccustomed to being in a place where a white man had just been executed. The sheriff announced there would be no public viewing of the body, by request of the deceased. After his announcement at about 4:30, the crowd began to disperse, looking for other entertainments.

That evening at Staub's Theater, after the vaudeville matinee was over, the famous actor John Drew and his 22-year-old co-star drew a big crowd with their Broadway sensation, the domestic comedy *My Wife*. The young beauty's performance as Beatrice Dupre captivated a *Journal* critic, who called her *fascinating*. "Billie Burke is a most attractive actress," he wrote. "She grows on the audience." That night in Knoxville, she stole the show from the more famous Drew.

I wonder how many people who saw Miss Burke on Gay Street that night recognized her 30 years later—when, in a whole new kind of cinematographic picture, a long one with color and sound, she played a character called Glynda, the Good Witch of the North.

In the 90 years since the promising young starlet performed at Staub's, no one has been executed in Knox County. Live theater no longer has that kind of competition.

—3/19/98

Casualty of War

America hadn't even joined the war that started the year before, but Knoxville newspaper readers were awed by the unbelievable body counts in Europe—more than half a million British dead already. Horrified, many were proud that Americans were too sensible to get involved in that ancient feud. But some were quoting philosopher William James's quip that war might be a less violent alternative to American football.

The Thursday night before they left for Nashville, the Vols hosted a "Jubilee," a very public scrimmage at old Wait Field, the sloping, gravelly gridiron at Cumberland Avenue and 15th. UT football was a club sport in 1915, rarely front-page news. In those days two private schools in Tennessee—Vanderbilt and Sewanee—ruled Southern football. No team had ever beaten both in the same season. No one, that is, until 1914, when these upstarts in the public college in Knoxville did and then took the Southern championship. The Vols suddenly had fans, literally hundreds of them.

Great things were expected for the 1915 season. By late October the Vols, led by quarterback Bill May, had a winning season, racking up 303 points in only four wins. The Vols' newest star was Bennett Jared, who'd scored two touchdowns in last Saturday's 101-0 win over Cumberland U. Some called the heavy-browed, earnest-looking young man from Buffalo Valley "Little Jared." Just 20, the substitute halfback was new to the squad, and smallish for a football player, but fast. Jared could run the hundred-yard dash in 10 seconds flat.

The University of Louisville's club, crippled by injuries, forfeited a scheduled Vols game. Multiple injuries in a single game were common in those days, when players wore only thin pads, sewn into their shirts, and thin leather headgear that did little to cushion hard licks.

Vol fans were supremely confident about the Vandy matchup, the Vols' biggest game of the year; local sportswriters declared it would be the biggest game in the South. Wagering was flagrant, with odds published in the local papers; some bookies were favoring the Vols by 10:7.

It was a "snappy practice session" on Wait Field that evening as the Vols went "through their signals with a rush that augurs ill for Vanderbilt." An addled *Sentinel* reporter gushed that "bubbles of enthusiasm are as plentiful…as mosquitoes in a willow swamp in September."

The Vols' young coaches, Zora Clevenger and his assistant, Miller Pontius, were less sanguine about their prospects. All Coach Pontius would allow is that "Tennessee is going at top speed now and we will certainly give Vandy a hard battle."

Vanderbilt had just beaten Ole Miss 91-0. Vanderbilt's speedy quarterback, "Rabbit" Curry, was notoriously hard to handle. Only 137 pounds, Curry was incredibly fast. Tackle Josh Cody was huge and tough. Dan McGugin, then the South's winningest coach, was in charge of a team reportedly hungry for revenge for last year's ruinous loss. Georgia Tech's coach, John Heisman—his name not yet associated with any trophy—was paying especially close attention to this game. Heisman predicted a Vanderbilt win.

Hundreds were on hand downtown at the Southern terminal to see the fearless Vol squad board the *Memphis Special* for Nashville. As the train passed near his hometown, just west of Cookeville, Bennett Jared likely bragged about Buffalo Valley to his teammates.

Preparing for the game in Nashville that Saturday, the Vols got a telegram: "Practically every businessman in Knoxville is awaiting the outcome," it went, "and depending on you to give a creditable account of yourself. You cannot serve your Alma Mater in a more profitable and beneficial manner than by winning this afternoon's game." It was signed the *Knoxville Board of Commerce*.

Fully 5,000 fans were at Nashville's Dudley Field to witness the struggle in person. Vandy ran onto the field to a loud cheer. As the Vols followed, a couple of them already limping—injured players got to play in those days—their Nashville hosts greeted the visiting Vols with a sportsmanlike "Rah! Rah! Rah!" Tennessee had an estimated 600 fans on hand, 350 of whom had arrived on another special train from Knoxville. They provided a "continuous din of yelling, singing, and applauding."

Meanwhile, back in Knoxville, fans went to the Bijou and paid a silver dime at the door. The theater had a telegraph connection to Nashville; an operator read the ticker-tape to give the audience the play-by-play and mark the action on a big board. Market Square had a similar setup. There would be little to cheer about.

Tennessee won the toss, but Vanderbilt scored early, on a 50-yard run by Rabbit Curry. Most of the first half was a defensive tug of war across the Vanderbilt field. Toward the end of the first half, it was still Vanderbilt 7, Tennessee 0.

Little Jared went in for halfback Bill Emory and assisted in a couple of plays, getting the ball to the 50-yard line. On first down, Jared carried for just a yard.

On the next play, May went back to fake a forward pass. Tommy Thomason ran past him as if to take the ball but instead blocked a Vandy player threatening May from the left. Jared, who'd been to May's left, took the ball and sprinted around to the right as if to make an end run. Vanderbilt closed the gap, though, and Jared chose to punch right though a narrow hole in the center. After he'd gained another yard, Vanderbilt players tackled him and piled on.

The referee called a water break. Everyone in the pile got up—everyone, that is, except Bennett Jared. His teammates carried out a bench as a stretcher and loaded him on. He said he couldn't feel anything.

As the fall afternoon darkened and rumors circulated about Jared's condition, UT lost what momentum it had. Vanderbilt won the game of the year, 35-0. The Commodores' last two touchdowns were scored in the dark, invisible to most of the spectators.

More than half of the Vols' players were injured that day. Vol tackle S.D. Bayer claimed that after one sack, the great Rabbit Curry took one furtive glance at the referee, then slugged Bayer in the face. Jim Luck sprained his ankle. Star Graham Vowell broke his and was expected to be out for the season, as were two other players. Bill May was described as "badly battered."

Nashville reporters had a good time describing the carnage. "There were mighty few gents who wore the orange and white who were able to lift themselves…without a twinge of pain shooting through some part of their anatomy," wrote one. Another observed that the Vols were "panting like a lizard and suffering several varieties of torture."

Sportwriters didn't mention that for Jared, one of those varieties of torture would be quadriplegia. When the team learned of his condition, UT canceled their following game with South Carolina and considered killing the rest of its season. But when it looked as if Jared might survive, they resumed the season. The Vols played two more games in 1915 but lost both, finishing the season 4-4.

Jared never returned to Knoxville. At his family home in Buffalo Valley, he recovered enough to get into a wheelchair occasionally and use his hands for small tasks. But he continued to have physical problems. In July 1917, as many of his old teammates enlisted to fight in Europe, Bennett Jared died. Brown Ayres, the 61-year-old president of UT, remarked, "I feel as if I would like never to hear of a football game again."

—11/6/97

Poisoning Domestic Animals

It's a curse. Every little scrap of phrase sends me into a reverie about some local gunslinger or scalawag. Walking past the Mercury Theater on Market Square this morning, I noticed some psycho-wacky posters for a fresh new pop duo out of Nashville, a married couple who call themselves Fleming & John.

Now, normal folks might be curious about these peppy, mod musicians and go down to the Mercury this weekend to give them a listen. Me, just reading their name got me thinking about a guy who died 96 years ago, an erudite hothead named John Fleming.

The Mercury's an old building. John Fleming himself likely walked past it hundreds of times, maybe even did a little jig there on the square the day his onetime mentor and manytime nemesis Parson Brownlow died.

They'd been friends and allies back before the War, though they made an odd couple. Fleming, 27 years Brownlow's junior, held a degree from Emory and Henry in Virginia. The Parson was originally from Virginia, but not the Emory and Henry neighborhood. As far as education, Brownlow never had much, but learned enough about the power of words to flay people alive.

Another thing that made them different was that the Parson didn't drink and didn't think anyone else should, either. But drinking was one of John Fleming's favorite hobbies.

In happier times Brownlow and Fleming headed up Knoxville's two most influential newspapers, both of them Whig rags. Their alliance on political issues, especially their support of the anti-Catholic Know-Nothing Party then sweeping the Northeast, was so cozy that Kingston editor Martin Patterson alleged that Fleming was a Brownlow puppet. The allegation so incensed Fleming, then only 23, that he confronted Patterson on Gay Street in front of the Coleman House (a.k.a. the Lamar House, now the front portion of the Bijou). What John Fleming did then was kick Patterson into the side of a passing cow.

During the War, the Parson was a Unionist; as his party dwindled, he turned Republican. Fleming was a Whig too, and a loyalist; but his fury at Republican Reconstruction made him a vengeful Democrat and an outspoken white supremacist.

The Parson and John Fleming became vicious rivals and enemies. By 1868 things had gotten so ugly between the two that they took to daydreaming in print about the death of the other. At the height of their morbid row, Fleming planted himself in a downtown saloon and enjoyed a binge of dimensions unusual even for him.

While the Parson worked his day job as governor of the state, his son, John Bell Brownlow, helped him with the *Knoxville Whig*, which dutifully reported Fleming's night on the town: "He was drunk from head to foot," went the story. "His feet were drunk and his legs were drunk and his Websterian brain was drunk. There wasn't a sober hair encircling his majestic brow."

Here you need to remember that in those days not only cows, but pigs as well, roamed wild downtown. (This wasn't just a Knoxville phenomenon, by the way. Just 20 years earlier, English visitor Charles Dickens was disgusted with the number of wild pigs roaming Broadway, in New York.) Anyway, Cox, the saloonkeeper, was uncertain about how to handle the delicate situation of a large, unconscious editor at closing time. "How to dispose of this very large elephant was a problem," was how the *Whig* put it. Cox considered "getting a handspike and rolling him out into the street …. But he knew that the hogs would eat him before morning, in which case the hogs would die, and Cox feared an indictment under the statute against poisoning domestic animals."

Cox hired two black men, at 50 cents each, to haul Fleming down Gay Street to Fleming's newsroom. They first objected "out of regard for their reputation," according to the *Whig*, and asked that next time the editor found himself too drunk to walk, Fleming "call on some good conservative of his own stripe, and not on respectable colored men."

The *Whig* wasn't quite finished, lending a final jab at Fleming's white-supremacist notions. "The colored people of Knoxville have been said to be ambitious to be ... the equal of the white man. If John Fleming is to be considered the representative white man, they now desire to be excused from equality with him, or those like him."

A lot of this, by the way, is in a spicy book by Steve Humphrey called *That D——d Brownlow*. Its title reflects an era when gentlemen were too delicate to spell out some words in print.

—*1/25/96*

Sut's Revenge

Somehow I knew right away who it was. Walking along the fire-escape side of the Bijou, I'd heard a rattling down at the basement opening and smelled some kind of chemical smoke when a skinny kid in what looked like a dirty nightshirt burst through, cussing at the splinters.

"Sut!" I shouted, as if I knew him. "Sut Lovingood!"

He seemed dazed, but then brushed off some soot and looked at me skeptically. "I see my repootashun reeks even further than the stink uv my carcass. But whar in God-damnation am I?"

"Why, this is old Knoxville, Sut," I said.

"The hell you say," he said, spitting a foul, 150-year-old plug of rabbit tobacco on the sidewalk. "Whar's the pigs?"

"I suppose they're eaten," I said. "Where have you been this past sesqui-century?"

"Oh, how you talk," he said with a sneer. "I shoulda knowed by yore shirt buttons that you was a prissy boy. Why, I been a-sojornin in Hell, vis-itin ole neighbors. But then I got *e-vick-tid*. Colonel Lucifer, he never did know what to do with me. Always got this corn-fused look on his big red face, like I had rascality so deep down under my hide that he knowed he didn't put it thar hisself. I speck I troubled him someway."

"Well, glad to have you back," I said, hoping I'd feel the same tomorrow. "Things have changed, I bet."

"Them auty-mobiles, I'd heard tell about," he said, surveying Gay Street. "But I never woulda figgered on that considerable iceberg, this far south."

"No, that's Jake Butcher's old bank," I corrected.

Sut brightened. "I heard tell o' Jake down yonder, too," he said. "Done us ol' boys proud." He peered around the corner. "Glad to see John Scherf's old saloon's still here."

"They call it the Bistro now," I said.

"Beast Roe? I don't know whar ol' John come up with that'n, but I am powerful thirsty." He shoved into what was once the Lamar House Saloon and sat at the near end of the bar. Several stools around him emptied. Sut ordered Lightnin'. The bartender thought he said "Lite." As the glass arrived, I bit my tongue. Sut took it down in one drag.

"They've cleaned up this Knoxville water since the last time I tasted it," he said.

"Modern folks call that beer," I corrected. I told him they did serve stronger stuff here. Sut got an eager look in his eye and baffled the bartender with orders for rawbone, blindeye, rednose, crackskull, splo. He finally settled for a vodka gimlet.

After his third or fourth, he slowed down long enough to talk. "I swar I almost got more questions than boils," he said. "Who's the one finally got to shoot the Parson?"

"Nobody," I said. "Parson Brownlow died an old man. Natural causes."

"You don't mean it. I had money on that'n. Speakin uv money, who's the quarterhorse champeen this month?"

"We don't have much of that anymore," I said.

"Wal then, who's yore bar rassler?"

"Bear-wrestling, cockfighting, snake-handling, eye-gouging—you pretty much have to cross county lines to find that kind of entertainment these days. Baseball, football, basketball—those are the games you see in the city now."

He looked at me blankly. "Prissy ball games in ol' Knoxville. I reckon yore fixin to tell me the ol' Flag Pond don't even stink no more."

"In fact it doesn't," I admitted. "They filled it in and built a railroad through it and developed it into a big wholesale commercial area. Then about a century later they developed it again into a place for bars and restaurants and shops."

"You know, I think I heard about some-a that from ole Kid Curry, the day he showed hisself. *The Bowery*, I think he called it."

"It's called the Old City now," I said. "It's a little different." I wanted to ask him what he knew about the fate of the Kid, but he was headlong on another track.

"You know, I never keered much for them stories George wrote about me," he said. Knoxville riverboatman George Harris immortalized Sut Lovingood in dozens of short stories popular in the 1850s and '60s.

"Why not, Sut?" I asked.

"Wal, it was partly cuz I couldn read em," he said. "I thought that was awful fancy of him, puttin them stories down on paper in them *readin* words. Ain't that a hell of a way to tell a story?"

"You know, you're not alone," I said. "Even graduate students have difficulty reading Harris's phonetic spellings."

"I ain't a bit sooprized," Sut said. "But the best stories I ever tole George I saved for the last. He put em in a new book called *High Times and Hard Times*."

I assumed he didn't know. "I hate to be the one to tell you this," I said. "That book is the one that's missing. George Harris had the only manuscript with him the night he died, right down Gay Street at the Atkin House. But then it disappeared. Nobody knows what happened to it. Nobody's ever even read it. People have been looking for it for 127 years."

Sut looked at his fourth empty glass and lowered his voice slyly. "George didn say nothin about bein pizened, did he?"

"Yes, that's exactly what he said—*poisoned*—and then he died." I looked at Sut, thinking maybe he knew something he wasn't letting on. "Tell me, how did you know that, Sut?"

He glanced at the bartender and mumbled, "I just spected that's the sorter thang George might say."

Wondering whether I should report this suspect in a long-unsolved murder, I took a hard draw on my Swanky. Were my loyalties with George or Sut? Writer or character?

Then, suddenly, Sut was off his stool, making friends with a receptionist. I figure he's already done his time.

—*9/11/97*

CHAPTER FIVE

JAZZ

Vine Street Drag

There's a big bronze-colored treble clef in the median at Gay Street and Summit Hill. The plantings aren't quite enough to block out the noise of heavy traffic from the interstate-style highway that's Summit Hill, but just enough to make it one of the most pleasant downtown nap spots for late-lurking winos.

At the base of the statue, in careful alphabetical order that doesn't allow for graceful additions, are inscribed the names of musicians. Lots of them are fine musicians, some of them great ones.

But there's one guitarist who's not on the list. He lived here longer, and was more intimately associated with this area, than most of those who are.

His name was Carl Martin. Born in southwestern Virginia 90 years ago this Monday, he and his dad, a former slave called Frank "Fiddlin'" Martin, moved to Knoxville when Carl was about 14 and already playing around with a guitar. With his brother in the '20s, Carl Martin played the downtown streets, medicine shows, and dances. Carl could dance, too, doing the buck-and-wing steps of which tap would be a more polite version.

Theirs was a string band: guitar, banjo, mandolin. The Martin brothers met a remarkable young fiddler from LaFollette named Howard Armstrong, who painted, played mandolin, and spoke Italian and several other languages he'd learned from immigrant friends in the area.

They called themselves the Tennessee Chocolate Drops.

By 1930, years before there was a Mid-Day Merry-Go-Round, the Drops were on live radio WROL here. Nervous the first time they played on the air, fiddler Armstrong missed his cue, then took off in the wrong key. The bassist tried to fill in by whistling, but choked on his chewing tobacco. Armstrong laughed as the band pulled into form. Everybody along Vine Street agreed it was the craziest intro they'd ever heard.

For a while the Martins and Armstrong even lived in the same house, on Yeager just east of downtown near the river.

Then they teamed up with a handsome young guitarist from South Carolina named Ted Bogan. The ladies called him "Mr. Black Gable." Renamed the Four Keys, they sounded like a jazzy, jumped-up country string band, maybe something along the lines of Django Reinhardt (who, incidentally, hadn't yet discovered jazz). Their no-rules string-band mania clocked at 250 beats a minute, except for the times that, for fun, they sped it up a little.

And at the old St. James Hotel on Wall, they cut their first records, "Knox County Stomp" and "Vine Street Drag."

Music writers speculate that Martin swapped licks with young guitarist Brownie McGhee, a teenager already playing professionally hereabouts. Besides Knoxville, they had one big thing in common: they made no clear distinctions between country and blues—because, maybe, there weren't any. In those days Uncle Dave Macon, Jimmie Rodgers, and all of the white founders of country were messing around with with black blues, while the Four Keys were doing stuff that often sounds a whole lot like bluegrass.

By 1933 they settled in Capone's Chicago, which was just developing its reputation for the blues. When black faces were still unfamiliar in that Midwestern metropolis, this Knoxville band's big advantage over the Mississippi bluesmen in town was that Armstrong could speak—and sing— in what he called "my Tennessee Italian."

Martin accompanied the greats Big Bill Broonzy and Tampa Red. His sound veered closer to the blues, which is what big-city types expected from black musicians anyway. He wrote topical songs that reflected the times: "Joe Louis Blues," "New Deal Blues," "1937 Flood." But he never forgot his roots in country and string-band music.

After service in World War II, Martin in middle age put his music to the side. But during the 1960s folk revival, he re-teamed with his elderly Knoxville pals to form Martin, Bogan, and Armstrong, which *Variety* called "America's last black string band." They were a strange creature touring American campuses. White students would pay to nod solemnly at weary, heavy-footed Delta blues and get instead something like bluegrass jazz with a jumpy fiddler and mandolinist who sang in Tennessee Italian.

Martin died in the late '70s. In 1985 Howard Armstrong, along with the considerably shyer Ted Bogan, became the focus of a remarkable documentary made by Terry Zwigoff. Partly filmed in LaFollette, it's named *Louie Bluie* (Armstrong's nickname) and is the funniest documentary ever aired on PBS. See it, but maybe not with your kids.

Today, if you look them up in the reference books, the categorizers who put Knoxville-bred Brownie McGhee in the "Piedmont Blues" camp tend to put Knoxville-bred Carl Martin and his cohorts over the "Chicago Blues" fence. Maybe they ought to try to build another fence just to hold the original Four Keys.

—3/28/96

Brownie McGhee, 1915-1996

I wasn't ready for the second time I ever saw him. It was opening day at the World's Fair, just after President Reagan left, and I was wandering through the crowded park with a kind of morbid curiosity.

On the Court of Flags I heard something different from the canned electronic disco that permeated the Fair: suddenly, wet, dirty, country blues. Two old men were sitting on one of those concrete steps, without furniture, without microphones, playing guitar and harmonica. The plaza swarmed with tourists, but only four or five people were watching this duo punching through the blues. People carrying handbags and wearing deely-bobbers walked above and around the old men, between them and their tiny audience.

The bearded guitarist wearing a floppy cap looked familiar. I knew I'd seen him somewhere, and the baldheaded harmonica player, too. I noticed the old man's bandoleer: tooled into the leather strap was the word SONNY.

"Hey!" I shouted. "This is Sonny Terry and Brownie McGhee!" Barely a year earlier I'd been among the thousands of paying customers who'd enjoyed their show at the Alumni Gym.

But here they were, incognito, at a splashy tourist bash. It was as incongruously strange as spotting Tolstoy at a Toyota Sellathon, or Jesus at a Christian Coalition fundraiser.

I had to tell somebody, so I started talking to strangers. Even if they didn't follow blues, I thought, they should know Brownie McGhee. He'd backed up everybody from Woody Guthrie to Paul Robeson to Harry Belafonte. He'd scored movies and had a prominent cameo in Steve Martin's recent comedy, *The Jerk*. A Van Morrison song paid homage to "Sonny Terry, Brownie McGhee, Muddy Waters...." It was, in fact, a music writer's reaction to a 1947 Brownie McGhee song that spawned the phrase *rock' n' roll*.

One guy sitting on the step next to them was about 20, with a gorgeous, incredibly buxom woman wearing extremely short pants, a woman I couldn't understand how he or any man could possibly deserve.

"Hey, man," this surfer dude said to Brownie. "You know any Rolling Stones?"

Brownie smiled at the sky. "No," he said. "Never met the boys."

I don't remember how long I sat there defying the flow of the tourists in splashy T-shirts who were obviously annoyed at this blues roadblock at their World's Fair. Brownie never seemed affronted. He'd started out playing the street, interacting with strangers. He'd stayed on the streets long after he had to, long after he was famous and successful. The Court of Flags wasn't much of a street, but he made the best of it.

A few others joined us that sunny spring afternoon, but I don't think there were ever more than 30 people there to hear one of Brownie McGhee's last performances in his hometown.

You might have read in Monday's *New York Times* that Walter "Brownie" McGhee died over the weekend in Oakland, California, where he spent the last several years of his life. He was born in Knoxville about 80 years ago, probably in the Lonsdale area, the son of a local street musician.

He grew up here and in Kingsport, Maryville, and Lenoir City. He learned on a guitar homemade from a wooden cigar box. He also played piano, jazz horn, banjo. For a blues guitarist, the repertoire he worked up at East Tennessee church picnics, juke joints, and medicine shows was unusually diverse. Some criticized him for spreading himself too thin, trying to please too many different audiences, as any working street musician must. But he knew that country and blues and folk and rock 'n' roll were just applesauce labels that retentive writers slapped on workingman's music they didn't always understand. If it had been up to him, country and blues would never have parted ways.

Sonny died several years ago, but Brownie kept going. He was in his 70s in 1986 when he had his biggest Hollywood role, co-starring with Mickey Rourke in the ultraviolent movie *Angel Heart* as a New Orleans voodoo man.

Last week I was looking into the story of the late blues guitarist Carl Martin. In the '30s, he helped build Chicago's reputation for the blues.

Martin lived in Knoxville in the '20s and early '30s, playing his blues live on local radio, and even cut a couple of sides here in Brownie McGhee's home town. One profile I found speculated the two probably knew each other in early '30s Knoxville, maybe swapped influences. "Why don't we just ask Brownie?" I thought.

About two months ago, a friend here in town who's a cousin of Brownie McGhee gave me his home phone number in Oakland. It's still there, pinned to my carrel wall. I think I was afraid I'd come across as another white boy asking dumb questions.

—2/22/96

Whoom, Like That

Near midnight on a November Friday in 1967, the university peninsula glowed with a homecoming bonfire for the championship-contending Vols. Upstream and across the river at Baptist Hospital, an elderly black woman died.

The following Sunday's *News-Sentinel* trumpeted news of the Vols' victory over Tulane and speculation that the Vols were the best football team in the nation. Also covered was the subsequent near-riot along Cumberland, which left one student critically injured with a fractured skull. But back on page C-7, the obituary page, appeared a small item about the woman who had died at Baptist that Friday night. This East Knoxville woman had been a dependable member of the choir at the Patton Street Church of God.

The same day that same woman got a much larger and more prominent write-up in the Sunday *New York Times*. And a week later, an obituary in *Time* magazine. After all, she may well have been the most famous person living in Knoxville in 1967.

Her name was Ida Cox. Forty years earlier, she was hailed nationwide as "the Uncrowned Queen of the Blues."

Though guesses at the year of her birth range across seven years, the *Guinness Encyclopedia of Popular Music* and other sources hold that Ida Cox was born in northern Georgia one century ago this month, on the 25th of February. She ran away from home as a child and sang comic roles in vaudeville-era minstrel shows. Her recording career began in 1923, the dawn of blues-recording history, when she cut a song called "Any Woman's Blues." She recorded about 70 other songs before the decade was over. In a day when few vocalists wrote their own lyrics, Ida Cox did. Hers were darker, bawdier, sometimes more sophisticated than most. One of her best-known, "Wild Women Don't Have the Blues," warns women never to treat men "on the square." A man won't cheat on a woman who keeps him guessing.

She spent most of her youth on the road, surviving three marriages. Though she didn't live here during her prime, she performed in Knoxville at least once, with one of her vaudeville revues, a memorable show at the legendary Gem Theater on Vine in 1931.

Over the years she sang with jazz immortals: King Oliver, Jelly Roll Morton, Louis Armstrong, Lionel Hampton. Blues Svengali John Hammond booked her in Carnegie Hall's 1939 extravaganza "From Spirituals to Swing," the show credited with popularizing boogie-woogie.

One night near the end of World War II, Ida Cox was singing at a nightclub in Buffalo, New York, when she collapsed. Though probably still in her 40s, she'd suffered a stroke. Sometime around 1950 she moved here to live with her daughter and recuperate. She would live in Knoxville longer than she had ever lived any one place in her life.

The woman once toasted by the jazz and blues elite of New York moved into a modest house on Louise Avenue and joined the Patton

Street Church of God. It became the most important thing in her life. Now that she was a churchgoer, she told those who asked, she didn't think it right to keep singing the blues.

Meanwhile, New York recording executives desperately tried to find her. In 1960, according to the *New Yorker*, Ida Cox "was located after a long search ... living in total obscurity in Knoxville, Tennessee." Riverside Records persuaded the reluctant Ida to visit Radio City Music Hall in April 1961 to record a final album. The *New Yorker's* "Talk of the Town" gushed: "Guess who was in and out of town last week, and after a 20-year absence, at that!" Describing her as "tallish, straight-backed, gray-haired, handsomely proportioned," the *New Yorker* interviewer observed she looked decades younger than her likely age. Talking about her upcoming session, Ida permitted no speculation about a comeback: "I mean to do the best I can," she said. "But then I'm going back home—*whoom*, like that."

With an all-star jazz band that included saxman Coleman Hawkins, trumpeter Roy Eldridge, pianist Sonny Price, and drummer Jo Jones, Ida Cox cut an album, *Blues from Rampart Street*, that was roundly praised for its rare quality.

And she never recorded again. She spent her last six years quietly in Knoxville. She lived barely long enough to witness "urban renewal"—and the eminent-domain condemnation of her home church. (Patton Street survives only as two sterile blocks east of the Old City. But Ida Cox's Louise Avenue home still stands.)

Her family buried her here in Knoxville at the Longview Cemetery on Keith. But that graveyard went out of business, and her daughter had her reinterred just across the ridge at New Gray Cemetery, off Western. With nothing to suggest her jazz-age glory, Ida Cox's small, plain gravemarker reads "Mother."

—2/5/96

The Moan

I was just finishing up a cover story, that Friday afternoon a few months ago, when I got a call from Scott Miller, the singer of the V-Roys. "Jack, Steve and I are down at the Bistro," he said. "He has something to ask you."

He didn't have to tell me Steve's last name, even though I'd never actually met the guy. I'd had an opportunity to meet Steve once, at a party at the brewpub, and had chickened out. I'd heard his records for years, seen him on TV. What could I have to say to one of the greatest singer/songwriters of our time?

I left the cover story in my boss's chair, 94 percent finished, and half-ran out the door, past Steve's name on the marquee of the Tennessee, to the Bistro.

I recognized him right away, of course: a big guy with longish hair and a T-shirt, drinking a glass of iced tea. He was sitting at the brick-lined Bistro like Jesse James, his back to the back corner. At his table were Scott and a couple of musicians who were touring with him.

I'd only barely shaken his hand when Steve Earle asked, "Where was the Arcade Building at?"

I stammered that the Arcade Building was still there, the old marble art-nouveau Journal Arcade not two blocks down the sidewalk on Gay Street, recently renovated. Steve said he'd seen that one and it wasn't the one. The Arcade Building he was looking for had burned down more than 60 years ago.

Steve had heard about the Arcade when he was on a recent tour of Europe—in Austria, I think he said. He'd heard about it in a song. He couldn't recall the name of the song, or the woman who sang it, but he said it was a great blues song about the fire that destroyed the Arcade Building in Knoxville.

I admitted I'd never heard of it, and I wondered if Steve was a little too innocent in his faith that there really was an Arcade Building in Knoxville that burned down; I suspected the song might have been about an Arcade Building in another city, Memphis, maybe, or that the place might have been altogether fictional.

I told Steve I was familiar with the popular-music sources, and I was sure I could find something.

I didn't find anything. But the other day I was surprised to spot my friend Nancy Brennan Strange up in the McClung Collection. I hadn't seen her up there before. You don't necessarily expect to find a popular nightclub chanteuse seated at a reading table in a genealogical library, not that there's anything wrong with that; but there she was. She was there trying to find what she could not about an ancestor but about a predecessor, a nightclub singer of the early 1930s named Leola Manning. Miss Manning's best-known song, recorded in Knoxville in 1930, was called "The Arcade Building Moan."

I dropped whatever I was working on and spent an hour or two trying to track down Leola Manning. All I could find about her was that she was a black woman who lived in East Knoxville from about 1927 to 1936—a different address every year, and not showing up at all a couple of those years. She apparently lived alone and worked for a time in the cafeteria of the old Mountain View school on Dandridge. Her name vanishes from the City Directory the year Bessie Smith died. Whether she moved or died or married, I don't know.

Her song has been on record at least a couple of times; once was when it appeared on a disc MTSU historian Charles Wolfe put together in 1982, *Historical Ballads of the Tennessee Valley*. According to Jubilee Arts' Brent Cantrell, who worked with Wolfe, Manning cut at least six sides at the St. James Hotel on Wall Avenue in the spring of 1930, part of Vocalion's near-legendary series of sessions there; Vocalion recorded everything from slick new jazz to rough-edged old-time hillbilly stuff on the mezzanine of the St. James.

For the past few weeks, cassette tapes of the "Moan" have been making the rounds among prominent local musicians. It's a blues: piano, guitar, and a rare voice sounding a little more polished than some of the Mississippi stuff of that era, a young, high, perfect voice—in opera you'd call it soprano—singing a long and detailed account of a fatal fire. *"Oh it was sad, sad, oh how sad / When the Arcade Building burnt down."*

Bridging the stanzas is a shy ad lib, in which Manning gives the song a title: *"What a moan in Knoxville."* The flip side of that 78 was called "Satan Is Busy in Knoxville."

But back to Steve's original question: through old newspapers and city directories, I learned where that Arcade Building was. It was on Union, at the other end of Market Square from the St. James. Just behind the Arnstein Building, in fact, where our offices are. The Arcade Building was a modest two-story walk-up that didn't even have a whole-number address: 410 1/2 Union Avenue, just 19 apartments, several of them vacant, but most of them occupied by white working-class families: a brakeman, a painter, an auto mechanic.

"On one Thursday morning, March the 20th day," the song goes, *"I think it was about two a.m..."* That was about when a gas explosion tore through the Arcade, blowing shards of glass into the windows across Union. The fire killed a family of three—a middleaged couple and a teenage boy. Another victim, a German immigrant named Carl Melcher, died nearby under mysterious circumstances (a story which deserves its own column).

According to Wolfe, Leola Manning sang her version of the story only 10 days after the fire—into a microphone right across the Square at the fireproof St. James.

Today the Arcade site is occupied by the much larger Grand Union building, which already looks old itself. But so far, I haven't run across any living person who recalls the humble Arcade Building—or the promising young blues singer who wrote its eulogy.

—7/9/98

Hot—and How!

As searchlights played the skies above the Andrew Johnson Hotel, six-foot loudspeakers blasted live music throughout a 20-square-block area of downtown, music with a fast tempo that had people jumping all the way to Market Square.

Back then, before Roy Acuff ever picked up a fiddle, home-grown Knoxville music was already making waves around the country, from New York to Chicago to Alabama. But this music getting national attention in 1929 wasn't country. It was music that had been a favorite in Knoxville for years. It was jazz.

Hundreds of local jazz musicians, black and white, played in various Knoxville venues, in park bandstands and vaudeville houses and dangerous nightclubs and country-clubs and posh hotel ballrooms, between 1900 and 1935. Most we'll never know by name. But one we do know, thanks in large part to several 78-rpm recordings he made in 1929 and 1930, relatively late in his career.

In 1996 a high-speed dance tune, "Postage Stomp," appeared on a compilation CD issued by Yazoo, called *Jazz the World Forgot* (Volume

1). It's a lighthearted but disciplined piece, with breaks for trombone and saxophone. A banjo played like a snare drum keeps the headlong tempo. The liner note mention it's a 1930 recording by a band led by one Maynard Baird. The CD publishers seem to know little about him except that he was based in Knoxville, Tennessee.

A genial man in his 60s is enjoying a comfortable retirement in a brick house overlooking a serene inlet of Fort Loudon Lake. He has a customized UT Vols mailbox, and a pickup truck in the front yard. He's a soft-spoken fellow, a retired electrical engineer for TVA. His name is Bob Baird, and he's bandleader Maynard Baird's son.

If you ask him, Baird will tell you about the guy playing banjo at 200 licks a minute on that cut. "I just barely remember my father playing on a bandstand on the top floor of the Andrew Johnson Hotel," he says. "It must have been 1934." Baird's mother—Maynard's second wife—had died when Bob was a baby, and until the elder Baird remarried, the boy often found himself hanging out with his dad and the other musicians. "He didn't have anybody to keep me," Bob says.

He knew his dad after his greatest fame, as a guy with a regular job who loved to tinker. But even in his workshop, his thoughts were never far away from music. Baird even invented a new instrument, which Bob describes as a cigar box with a broom handle attached: the Baird-ola. It sounds fascinating.

"Well, I think I've got one in the basement," he says, getting up. He returns with an almost-handsome, carefully crafted instrument, several stages beyond the cigar-box stage, with fiddle slots and a single string, now hanging loose, which was to be played with a bow.

Today Bob is the Keeper of the Baird-ola and of a thick scrapbook of clippings, letters, photographs, fliers, and dance cards, covering the years 1926 to 1930, the height of Baird's popularity.

"My older brother remembers him a lot better than I do," he says.

His brother, Maynard Baird, Jr., is in fact 18 years older than Bob. When he blew trumpet in Knoxville in the '30s, he was known as "Sonny" Baird. Today he lives outside of Camp Pendleton, in California. His 33 years in the U.S. Marine Corps spanned active duty in three wars. He still keeps a military schedule, and asks to be called at 6:00 a.m., Pacific time.

He tells his father's story.

Maynard Baird was born in Memphis around 1895; Sonny says nobody knows the date for certain. Like many musicians, his father was vague about his age and never celebrated birthdays. He spent his early youth in the Memphis of W.C. Handy's early days—but by 1913, for reasons now forgotten, the teenage Baird was in Knoxville, working as a vaudeville musician and movie-show operator. During the slow transition from vaudeville to movies, theaters showed both on the same ticket, and a successful movie operator had to entertain. Baird learned quickly.

He could play nearly everything, they say: piano, banjo, drums, harmonica, sometimes several at once, novelty one-man band shows. He fell for local piano player Mae Adams. Sonny was born in Knoxville in 1915, when his dad was only 20; he says his parents were on tour at the time, on their way to Cincinnati.

In 1921, Baird formed the first version of his best-known band, the Southland Serenaders—a large jazz combo with cornets and saxophones that made room for his own banjo, and, sometimes, jazz fiddle. He and his young family lived like gypsies, touring and keeping a dozen different Knoxville residences in as many years.

Sonny was only 7 when his dad bought him a cornet at a local pawnshop. Around 1924 Baird divorced Sonny's mother, who then moved to Montgomery, Alabama. "He was quite a ladies' man, in his younger days," says Bob. The bandleader married at least three times; his sons say there may have been more to it than that.

Baird spent much of the decade touring, playing his own compositions and the pop standards of the day: "St. Louis Blues," "Tiger Rag," "Blue Heaven," "Yes She Do!," and the Charleston classic, "Paddlin' Madeline Home." He was a habitual entrant in battle-of-the-bands musical competitions; in 1925, playing a casino in New Jersey, Baird entered one more, and won. Among the rivals he bested was a band fronted by pop star Rudy Vallee.

Baird toured widely, but Knoxville saw him more than anybody else. His hometown wasn't necessarily limiting. Baird's live audiences at Whittle Springs and elsewhere sometimes approached 2,000. And by the mid-'20s, the city was getting a reputation for its powerful radio station,

WNOX, which could be heard over much of the eastern half of the country. Baird's performances on WNOX's show "Midnight Frolic" from 1926 to 1928 drew an astonishing array of fan mail from Pittsburgh, Chicago, South Bend, small-town Pennsylvania: "the best band in the air" they called Maynard's Serenaders.

A letter from Woodbury, New Jersey, described the Serenaders as "one of the finest dance orchestras I have ever listened to...your only fault is...that you signed off too early." (The "Midnight Frolic" signed off at 3:10 a.m.) Baird's best radio fan mail may have come from Norfolk, Virginia. "I thought the old Radiola would have a short circuit, for your station has the live wires," wrote a fan in 1928. "I mean the boys played hot—and how."

Baird headlined various prime-time radio shows over the years: the "Style Shop Hour," "Tradin' Claude's Studebaker Program," "McClung's Radio Frolic." Baird also played on another station with reach— Nashville's WSM, not yet famous for its new Saturday-night variety show, the "Grand Ole Opry."

At several regular stops Baird was treated like a superstar: Waldameer Beach Park, in Erie, Pennsylvania, where he sometimes shared a bill with the great black bandleader Fletcher Henderson; Luna Pier, in Lakeside, Michigan, (alongside a young Duke Ellington); an Ohio nightspot called Greenwich Village, "Dayton's Smartest Supper Club." In ads for these shows, Maynard's Southland Serenders sound almost exotic: "The Hottest and Sweetest Band in the South," "The Versatile Sensation of Dixie," "Dixie's Hottest Dance Band." One bill hailed them as "America's Greatest Collegiate Orchestra." Perhaps that's one reason Baird was vague about his age and background; at the time he fronted "America's Greatest Collegiate Orchestra," Baird was well into his 30s, and no college boy. (He sometimes introduced Sonny as his kid brother.)

"Dad had a lot of ham in him," says Bob. "He was almost cocky." In 1929 Baird rode in an airplane over Huntsville, Alabama, and carpeted the city with leaflets advertising his show at nearby Monte Sano. It made headlines in the Huntsville newspapers: "The Modern Way to Advertise."

"I wish I had some of those traits," says his modest son Bob. "They left me out."

Baird played extended engagements of weeks at a time but seemed to have the busiest band in his hometown, too, hosting Charleston contests at the Bijou Theater and "Surprise Revues" at the Riviera.

Modern musicians know the phenomenon of being least appreciated at home. The only negative comments Baird saved in his scrapbook came from the Knoxville papers. After a 1926 gig at the Riviera, a conservative reviewer for one of the dailies sniffed, "The music was all right, we suppose, for those who like the sort of tinpanny tantrum modern orchestras are supposed to put out." Of a later show there, a reviewer wrote, "Members of the band would be better if they would devote their exclusive time to playing and cut out the attempted comedy."

The comedy bit somehow worked much better up North. According to an Erie newspaper, the band kept the large crowds at the Waldameer "in a constant roar of interest and excitement," even when they were just "dancing or grouped chummily around a table."

The Serenaders often featured a full variety show, with music, comedy, and dancing. As a boy, Jack Comer (later owner of Deane Hill Country Club) danced with the band in a bellhop outfit—the Charleston, of course. Lillian Law, an exotic dancer and contortionist from Chicago, also performed with the Serenaders. Joe Fox was billed as an "eccentric dancer" and "clown drummer." For a time the Serenaders toured the nation with movie star Helen Munday, promoting her Tennessee-based silent, *Stark Love*.

Jazz was dance music and purely entertainment. "In those days, there was Kansas City-style jazz, New Orleans jazz, Chicago jazz, all just a bit different," recalls Sonny. "Most of Knoxville's jazz musicians, and my dad, leaned more toward the Kansas City type than anything else."

Baird advertised his band as "10 Musicians—30 Instruments," but his bands ranged in size from about 8 to 15 members; more than 30 local musicians were official Serenaders at one time or another. Baird's brother-in-law, Vic Johnston, was billed as "King of the Ivories." Another pianist, Ralph Maloney, was "the Prince of Jazz." Saxman Bugoo Gallaher was "One Ton of Fun." Among the stars was Sammy Goble, "Dixie's Sweetest Trumpeter" and a veteran of Paul Whiteman's seminal big-band orchestra; he taught Sonny to play. Another trumpeter, Jerome Licht, went on to play for Ray Miller's popular New York-based band. Perhaps the most famous musician ever to play in Baird's band was the legendary jazz violinist Joe Venuti. Sonny recalls the Italian-born Venuti—who played in a style only later associated with Stephane Grapelli—was in Knoxville for a time as a member of the Serenaders.

In 1926 the Southland Serenaders were invited to New York to make the first recordings at "Brunswick Recording Laboratories" for Vocalion. It's unclear what became of those experiments. But in 1929 Vocalion set up a recording studio at the old St. James Hotel, near Market Square. Most of what they recorded there was country music, but they cut a few jazz records, too—among them tunes by the Tennessee Chocolate Drops, the maverick string-jazz band; and Maynard's Southland Serenaders. Sonny remembers the studio. "During those days, they only had one microphone, and, of course, there was no mixing."

Maynard Baird's first two Vocalion records, each bearing two songs, were released on October 15, 1929. It's unknown whether the Crash that followed only two weeks later was a decisive factor in his career.

In late 1929 a new venue opened in downtown Knoxville: Advertised with searchlights, one rotating, and the other fixed on McGhee Tyson Airport (then located in Bearden) to direct aeroplane traffic in those pre-radar days, it was the fabulous new Andrew Johnson Hotel. Baird and the Serenaders signed on as the hotel's house band, playing in the Crystal Ballroom and broadcasting on WNOX from the Venetian Room. The Serenaders gave two supper-dance shows a week at the AJ. Shows were broadcast over the airwaves and from "mighty" loudspeakers on top of the building. They say you could hear it for six blocks around.

According to that CD's liner notes, "Postage Stomp" was recorded in 1930—again, probably, at the St. James.

The scrapbook ends in 1930, and you get the impression the jazz-age decade of the Southland Serenaders was about over, too. Maynard Baird kept playing, but kept changing personnel and names: Maynard's Syncopators, Maynard's Southern Foot Warmers, Maynard Baird and his Southern Gentlemen. A handbill from those days is poignant: "REGARDLESS OF THE DEPRESSION," it reads, "THIS ATTRACTION WILL DRAW THE CROWDS TO YOUR DANCES LIKE [a] MAGNET."

Maybe it did, but Baird apparently didn't travel as much in the '30s. "Making a living in the music business was not easy in those days," says Sonny. Bob recalls growing up on Oklahoma Avenue with an old school bus in the driveway, ready to take to band wherever they were called. A description of one Newport gig in 1937 is tucked into the scrapbook. Sonny says his dad was still getting royalties for his recordings in the late '30s; he doesn't know when they stopped.

In the '30s, some old jazz stars—who a decade earlier had worn tuxedoes behind monogrammed podiums—put on overalls to play country music for WNOX or WROL. "It was a jazz band that played at that 'Mid-Day Merry-Go-Round,'" says Sonny. "See, it was more steady work. So they played country in the day and jazz at night."

By 1938 Maynard Baird was turning his attention to the labor movement. His sons say he got involved in it through the Knoxville Musician's Union, and advertised his band as a union band. The bandleader once famous in Ohio as "that Great Big Man from the South" ran for Knoxville City Council in 1939 but lost. Neither son knows for sure why he gave up jazz, but popular music had changed. Swing was smoother, without as much of the high-speed hot-footed dance music of the Jazz Age. The prominent swing bandleaders were younger than Baird. In his 40s, Baird may have been getting a little long in the tooth for the lifestyle.

His erstwhile "little brother," Sonny, wasn't. As a teenage trumpeter, Sonny joined Stan Stanley's orchestra, based in West Palm Beach, Florida. Then he was back home in Knoxville playing for Bob Lavin's band. In 1938, when Lavin enlisted in the army, 23-year-old trumpeter Sonny stepped up to lead the band. "We were quite popular down Kingston Pike way," he recalls. "It was a hotty-totty area in those days. All the clientele at Cherokee Country Club wore tuxedoes and tails." Although he says they were "more a society band" than his dad's had been, Sonny was still good enough to be occasionally invited to sit in as a trumpeter down at the black nightclubs of Vine Street.

In 1942 Sonny enlisted in the Marines, fully intending to return home and resume his career as a jazz trumpeter. Fate had other plans. "On the Okinawa operation, I got hit by a mortar round," he says. "It took my teeth and jawbone out." Plastic surgery fixed him up, and today the 83-

year-old Baird speaks without impediment. Still, "it ended my trumpet-playing days." Without jazz to return to, he stayed in the Marines, good for a tour in Korea and three tours in Vietnam before he retired. He still leads a military life in his home outside Camp Pendleton, up every morning at 5:00 sharp. He's now regional commander of the Military Order of the World Wars, a combat veterans' group.

Meanwhile, Maynard Baird lived a quieter, more practical life than he had before, but he stayed close to the music business, occasionally coaxed out of retirement to play with old cronies at a country-club dance. In the '50s he fashioned a recording studio out of his home on East Fifth, making tapes and cutting records for Jerry Collins and the big bands that remained. The man who led Knoxville's hottest band of the Jazz Age died in Knoxville in 1965, identified in the news stories mainly as a union leader.

His third wife, the young singer he married in the '30s, still lives in Florida, but Baird's sons believe all of the old Serenaders are gone. Perhaps the last surviving member, drummer Joe Parrott, a neighbor of Bob's in Concord, died only last year, in his 90s.

Two of Baird's surviving 78s, "Postage Stomp" and "Sorry" are listed in record-collectors' guides at $50 each. Both brothers have copies of "Postage Stomp." "Mine is so scratchy I can hardly hear it," says Sonny. They don't know who owns the rights, and don't seem to worry about it. Bob has bought out all the local record stores' copies of *Jazz the World Forgot* and has more on order. He and his brother are just grateful, after 70 years, to have a clean copy of the music that for one enchanted decade unlike any other, made their father famous.

—4/9/98

CHAPTER SIX

MODERN HISTORY

Kohlrabi, Muscadine, and Cushaw

In 1853, when they donated Market Square to be used as "a curb market for farmers forever," Joe Mabry and William Swan were young, vigorous men. Still, neither would live to see the construction of what we call "the old courthouse," or our old train stations, or our oldest theater, or the oldest of downtown Knoxville's chapels. In 1853 the Old City wasn't even New yet. Mr. Mabry and Mr. Swan wouldn't recognize any of that stuff, because none of it was there in the Knoxville they knew.

But they would recognize Market Square—and at harvest time they'd probably drop by long enough to say howdy to Sherrill Perkins.

He wears clean bluejean overalls and a green Price's Landscaping cap. His grandfather sold here in the 1800s; his father sold here in the '20s. Perkins isn't sure how long he's been coming here himself, three days a week—10 years, maybe 12. Other farmers sell nearby, but none with the selection or regularity that Perkins does.

He unloads early on Mondays, Wednesdays, and Fridays. By then he's already done his chores at his farm on the French Broad, loaded up his homegrown stuff, and visited the wholesale produce markets on Forest Avenue, partly to buy bananas, which don't grow well on the French Broad, and partly to check on this week's fair prices. Then he drives up to Mabry and

Swan's old Market Square and sets his goods out on the counters underneath the shed at the north end. It takes nearly an hour just to put it out: dozens of varieties of produce, three or four varieties of fresh tomatoes from his own farm, several kinds of fresh greens, beans, corn, peppers, squash, and root vegetables, bananas and peanuts from the produce markets on Forest, going cheaper than you can get them in the stores. Honey, jellies, apple butter. Hot chow-chow, pickled okra, and cucumbers that Perkins's 82-year-old aunt cans in Mason jars, cakes she bakes and wraps in cellophane.

Perkins doesn't even know how many different crops he grows. "I've never counted," he says. "The meat, that's my biggest drawing card." It surprises people from the sanitary suburbs to see unrefrigerated ham, poke sausage, and salt pork sitting on a wooden shelf alongside the squash and bananas and hot peppers. Perkins also raises hogs on his farm, cuts and salts down this meat himself, cures it so well it doesn't even need refrigeration.

Start picking stuff up and Perkins will sling open a small paper bag from his stack and hand it to you. He's got a fan he hasn't plugged in today, a watering can to keep his greens moist, a 10-pound scale hanging from a rope. He has plastic chairs but doesn't sit much. Others do. Perkins always appears to have a big support staff, older guys who greet customers as they approach. They sometimes get up to sprinkle some water on the greens. But they're just guys from the Square, happy to have company.

There's a steady stream of customers this Friday morning. Some buy one thing, a tomato or a banana, and eat it on the spot. Others buy in bulk, like greens for church picnics.

Perkins is patient with the ignorant. On his top shelf is a large green-striped gourd the size and shape of Popeye's right arm. Perkins calls it a cushaw; he allows that some folks pronounce it *cutshaw*. "You make pies with it," he says.

In season he carries other exotics: kohlrabi, Chinese radishes, Korean radishes, and, today, muscadine. "The other day, a lady bought four boxes of muscadine. I said, 'You gonna make some jelly?' She said, 'No, I'm gonna eat them. I'll eat the best part of them tonight.'"

His prices and his selection draw everybody. An old lady, perhaps 80, struggles painfully toward the counter, taking six-inch steps with the help of her cane.

"You movin' awful fast this mornin'," Perkins says.

"They call me Whizbang," she says.

He's selling lots of greens today. Just 10 a.m., and he's sold 10 of the 14 bushel baskets he brought, at $18 a bushel. Most of the growing season's coming to a close, but this is still greens season, fresh new crops of turnip and mustard greens in tall skinny baskets that look like congas.

A skinny, emphatic man is rummaging through Perkins's boxes of bananas: "You *spose* to keep some green ones *and* some ripe ones, and you got the green ones, but you ain't got no ripe ones, not a one."

Perkins moves with slow confidence to the banana boxes, picks up a few bunches, and finds the man a couple of ripe bananas.

"My grandfather lived to be 100 years and seven months," Perkins says. "He smoked a pipe, dipped snuff, took a drink at night. I asked my doctor about that. He said people his age, they got more exercise than we do. On a busy day, though, you just all day long waitin' on people, you think you get plenty exercise."

About 100 people have been through here in an hour. A young black man picks up a small Romano tomato.

"How much for one?" he asks.

"Eighty cents a pound," Perkins says. He puts the one small, lonesome tomato in the hopper. He squints. "Here, take two, and make it half a pound."

"You wouldn't have some salt, would you? I like 'em with salt."

"Yeah." Perkins reaches over for a cardboard saltshaker that's marked PEPPER and from it he pours a double tablespoon of salt into the other man's open hand.

"You don't want to kill me, do you?" says the customer. Perkins grins in the way of people careful not to spill their chew. The customer dips one tomato in his palm and eats it whole.

"The main thing is to be nice to people," Perkins says. "A little politeness don't hurt nothin."

You can't stay in business for 144 years without it.

—9/25/97

Downtown Stadium In

Last Wednesday morning, through the window of a *News-Sentinel* box on Market Street, I saw the headline, "Downtown stadium out," and wondered. Downtown merchants had been hopeful that a baseball stadium behind Gay Street would be just the magnet that would finally bring hungry and thirsty Knoxvillians downtown again. The Smokies, feeling their current site is too remote, were also pushing for the move, convinced a downtown location would bring bigger crowds to the games, too.

At lunchtime, I decided to see just how remote from downtown Bill Meyer Stadium is. I'd driven there from home a hundred times but had never attempted the journey from downtown.

Given the fact that I'm pushing 40 and don't get any regular exercise, maybe I should have hesitated to try such an expedition without some preparation. But on a reckless impulse, I laced up my best $9 pair of Converse All-Stars, filled up my canteen, checked my compass, packed a topographical map, and set out from the Old City, just to see if I could make it all the way to the ballpark.

I never got to open my canteen. That hike from Lucille's to the front gate of Bill Meyer Stadium took 12 minutes.

There's sidewalk the whole way and, unlike some parts of downtown, no appreciable hills involved. If you get hungry during that 12-minute trek, there's the plate lunch at Smoky's Cafe and barbecue at Dixson's. To avoid boredom during the longer stretches, I looked at lots of interesting stuff along the way. There's the big marble marker on the sidewalk across Randolph Street from Chicken City, inscribed *He lived humbly but died nobly,* a monument to a heroic street scavenger who died while trying to stop a runaway Harrison's truck in 1964. There's Florida Street, which was once Knoxville's red-light district (though it takes some imagination to picture that today). Over on East Jackson, there's the small, fancifully decorated chapel called "The Singing Church." On East Depot, there's the famous New Knoxville Brewing Company *and* the Knoxville Opera Company, both in relatively new digs; and on Morgan, the intimidatingly big turn-of-the-century headquarters of the AFL-CIO. It turned out to be 12 of the most enlightening minutes of my week.

I unfolded my map. "Hunh," I said. "Our ballpark's *already* downtown." Measuring distances on the map with my thumbnail, I discovered the present baseball stadium is less than half a mile from Jackson and Central. Bill Meyer Stadium is a little closer to the Old City than the mayor's office is.

It's been downtown for as long as anybody remembers. It had to be, because when they established it at Caswell Park, around the corner from Gay Street, circa 1920, most people didn't drive cars.

Modern transportation technology is supposed to shorten distances, but sometimes it seems to lengthen them. Lots of folks today assume the ballpark's much farther out than it is—even some loyal Smokies fans are sometimes surprised to hear it's only a few blocks from the Old City.

It somehow got farther away when they built the interstate. The exits off the James White connector seem to encourage you to get there without glimpsing any of the familiar parts of downtown, and the elevated parkway itself, though it doesn't actually impede foot or automobile traffic, forms an invisible curtain in some people's minds, some psychological barrier they fear to cross.

To be fair, I have to admit that before last week, I've rarely found cause to take that particular stroll. (I did once walk all the way from Whittle Communications to the Unemployment Office farther out on Magnolia, but that's another story.) Dominated by loading docks, that northeastern sector of downtown is no garden spot, and with the possible exceptions of the Opera and the premium brewery, it's not necessarily upscale.

But the shortness of the stroll did get me wondering what *is* downtown, exactly, and why this section that includes Bill Meyer Stadium—and the brewery, and the opera company, and the AFL-CIO—isn't part of it. This neighborhood definitely *looks* urban: two, three, and four-story-buildings fairly close together, a diverse variety of businesses, sidewalks everywhere. It's more densely used than some officially sanctioned parts of downtown. Almost all of the buildings I saw appeared to be well occupied. It gets you to thinking that back when Knoxville was a big city, back before the interstates and urban renewal, heck, maybe this *was* downtown. Maybe it still is.

—3/6/97

Paradox in the Stars and Bars

Let's say you're a 16-year-old white supremacist. You don't like blacks and you don't like Jews. You do like the Nazi swastika because it looks real scary—but then, it reminds you of foreigners, and you don't like foreigners. So your favorite symbol is American, the Rebel flag.

Well, hang on tight, kids. Here's some stuff they don't teach you in third grade.

If you like to be around mostly white Anglos, you might not like the Confederate States of America very much. In 1861 the C.S.A. may well have been the most racially diverse nation in the northern hemisphere. (That's the top half of the globe, kids.)

We don't have space to get into the stories of Judah P. Benjamin, the Jewish senator who was the Confederate secretary of state *and* secretary of war (some Northern abolitionists charged that secession was a Jewish plot!). Or Stand Watie, the Cherokee who was the most defiant Confederate general, the very last to surrender. Or the thousands of Confederate Cajuns and Hispanics from Texas and Louisiana that you can see in old pictures, wearing Confederate serapes.

And we don't have to go that far away to find something that'll make you scratch your bald head. You wouldn't have known what to make of some of the things a guy who used to live on the downtown end of Cumberland Avenue said. His name was Parson Brownlow, and he was a Unionist *and* a white supremacist. Parson Brownlow really, really hated the Confederacy—partly because it was full of black people! Parson Brownlow called the Confederacy "the Niggerdom." See, he thought it was really gross, the Confederate habit of eating at the same table with blacks and attending black dances. The parson said, let's get rid of the Confederacy, kill everybody in it, black and white both.

He was such a strong Union man that he was invited to have supper with Lincoln. He later became Reconstruction governor of Tennessee. But here in Knoxville, before the Union army arrived, the Confederates threw him in jail and talked about how they'd kill him.

Now, the Parson was a very strange guy who had a whole lot of problems, but if you look at him sideways, he sort of had a point. Any way you want to measure it—in the way we talk, the food we eat, the music we play—the okra-eating, banjo-playing "Confederate" South has been strongly influenced by African culture. Maybe more so than has any other European or American white culture in history.

Now, don't get me wrong. I don't want to turn one annoying oversimplification into another one. I'm not one of those who will tell you slavery had nothing to do with the war, or that most Confederate officers were freedom riders before their time. There were about a hundred-odd paradoxes about slavery and race, but slavery was at its core a racist institution, and the C.S.A. condoned it. Mostly.

I say *mostly*, kids, because I found out that toward the end of 1863, the same year the Emancipation Proclamation was enacted, one General Patrick Cleburne, C.S.A., was putting together a interesting proposal.

Cleburne was a fierce Southern patriot who'd spent several days in Knoxville in 1862, organizing an invasion of Kentucky (which was then a pro-Union slave state—had you heard about that?). About a year after he was here, Cleburne wrote his own proposal for emancipation: "We can do this more effectively than the North can now do, for we can give the Negro not only his own freedom, but that of his wife and child, and we can secure it to him in his old home. To do this, we must immediately make his marriage and parental relations sacred in the eyes of the law and forbid their sale…we would do best to make the most of it…by emancipating the whole race upon reasonable terms."

Not even President Lincoln was ready to go that far. After all, four important slave states didn't join the Confederacy, and the Emancipation Proclamation excused them. The president didn't want to upset loyal Unionist slaveholders during wartime.

Cleburne showed his proposal to his friends and colleagues. Six Confederate generals and several other Rebel officers approved Cleburne's plan with their signatures. But in January 1864, their superior, General Joseph E. Johnston, said no. He didn't say, "No, you're fired," or "No, what are you doing in this army, you dang abolitionist traitors." He just said it sounded like a matter for the civilian government. More than a year later, in the last months of the War, the Confederate legislature passed a watered-down version of it, offering freedom to those who fought for the South.

Patrick Cleburne and Gen. John Kelley, one of the other Confederate generals who signed Cleburne's proposal, might well have protested to the legislature in favor their original idea, to free everybody in the Confederacy, and maybe save the Confederacy by doing so.

They might have, but by then they were dead. They had been killed by

Union bullets at Franklin in late 1864 while fighting under that Rebel flag.

So, if you wave the Rebel flag thinking it's a symbol for some weird, old ideas that still scare some people today, you're right. But it's more mixed-up than that, isn't it?

The Civil War was a complicated war, and people had about a million different reasons for wanting to fight for one side or the other. But don't trouble your shaved head trying to figure it all out!

If you want a war that's black-and-white simple and easy to understand, try *Star Wars*. It's a movie that came out a long time ago, before you were born. I bet you'd like it!

—9/10/93

Deane Hill

Maybe I don't get out to West Knoxville as much as I should. But I had a business lunch in Downtown West a couple of weeks ago, and driving back on Gleason Road approaching Morrell, I came across a startling barren landscape, like a ridge on Uranus.

It took a minute to realize that this red-clay desert was about where Deane Hill Country Club used to be.

I hadn't been to Deane Hill in a long time. The last time was nearly 20 years ago, when I was majoring in something or other at UT and an attractive girl I'd met at the Last Lap invited me to a sorority dance at Deane Hill. It was a rare opportunity for me or any other guy who spent his Saturday nights alone drinking longnecks at the Last Lap.

We went in my Karmann Ghia and parked in the boxwood-lined parking lot and went inside this old place. But once we were on the ballroom, Ellen made it clear that she had no intention of actually dancing. She sat and talked with her friends, while I wandered around this grand old house I hadn't seen since I was a kid.

Back before West Town, back when you could hear cattle mooing on this hill, my family went to Deane Hill to swim. It was cheaper than most country clubs, especially for folks like us who promised never to use the golf course. In those days, when even our rich friends didn't have pools in their backyards, Deane Hill must have been the only swimming pool we had access to.

We'd leap barefoot out of the Fairlane wagon, hot-foot it across the parking lot, and race down the long tree-shaded walk between the house and the boxwoods, impatient with how slowly moms can walk. We'd round the right turn at the end of the walk, then the left, and we'd know we were almost there. From the crest of that hill, down the grand concrete stairway before us, was a sudden vista of delight.

Invisible from the road, a discreet distance down the hill from the house, surrounded by woods and rose gardens, was the best swimming pool in the world. From there you couldn't see any cars, or parking lots, or steel fences. On summer Saturdays the pool was so crowded there was no actual swimming going on. It was a big half-submerged party: Marco Polo and cannonballs and kids begging their moms to come on in. But the moms all seemed content to line up in deck chairs smeared with aromatic Coppertone, reading *Dr. Zhivago*.

There was a snack shop at the south end of the cabana, with a patio overlooking the eastern slope, tall trees growing up alongside it, like a scene in an old Japanese painting. The first time I ever ordered something for myself, and paid money for it, was from that window, right there. ("I want a hot dog," I said to the guy, who reminded me of a bartender in a movie. "Do you want that with everything?" the guy asked. An unexpected dilemma. I considered running back to Mom. "Sure," I said.)

The big, dark-paneled rooms in the old house at Deane Hill hinted at the mysteries of adulthood. When liquor-by-the-drink was still illegal in Knoxville, Deane Hill had a real bar, with a real bartender like in the movies. I sometimes caught glimpses of it, men in jackets and narrow ties, a grown man's place with an unexplainable language of highballs and cocktails. For years that was my only image of a real bar in Knoxville.

On Wednesday nights I put on a jacket and clip-on tie—because I was told that men were not allowed into Deane Hill after 6:00 without a jacket and tie—and my mother and grandmother and an old man called Mr. McKee would go to Deane Hill, which was a completely different place after dark. There, in the foyer by the staircase that wound up to the unknown second floor, was a basket of square cards printed BINGO. I chose mine carefully.

The place was usually crowded with elegantly dressed gray-haired people I imagined to be professors and barons and ambassadors. I don't remember other kids. There, at age 8, I would have regarded other kids with disdain.

We always sat in a corner room near the back, with windows onto the ballroom. With bookcases and stuffed chairs and ottomans, it looked like an elegant private parlor. I was careful to get down off my big chair and stand whenever a lady came into the room. I was told that was a very important thing for a young man to remember, and for the rest of my life, people would know that I was a gentleman. At Deane Hill adulthood was cryptic and complex, an elusive state of perfection.

The place was changing by the time we quit, the old-fashioned marble and dark-wood ballroom remodeled to look more like a suburban-chic restaurant.

I wasn't there for another decade—but for those years, without thinking, I would read books and picture the action at old Deane Hill. The spooky old house in the Hardy Boys' *While the Clock Ticked*. The gentleman's club in *Around the World in 80 Days*. The ballrooms in Fitzgerald's *This Side of Paradise*.

Back there for that one night, at that sorority nondance 20 years ago, I drank gin and roamed alone around the house, wearing the jacket and tie that were apparently no longer required. It was smaller than the palace I remembered, but I still knew my way around. When I returned to the ballroom, Ellen seemed embarrassed about how talkative I was getting to be. She insisted on driving back to campus. I don't think we went out again.

I've never gained admittance to that distinguished adult world that I prepared myself for at Deane Hill 30 years ago. And now, Deane Hill has vanished from the earth.

—9/4/97

Student Unrest

As I write this, my son is in our nation's capital, doing the same sort of thing I was doing when I was his age.

In the late spring of 1970, during the student strike just after the U.S. bombing of Cambodia, I got on a bus and went to Washington with dozens of other like-minded students. We just wanted to be *part of it* for a few days, and see what there was to see.

But everywhere we went, doors were closed in our faces. They asked us to leave the Capitol Building, wouldn't let us through the White House gates, wouldn't even let us into the Smithsonian.

There were thousands of long-haired protesters at the Lincoln Memorial, hanging out on the lawn, wading naked in the reflecting pool. Everywhere cars were turned upside down, burning. We got in trouble, too, for one thing and another.

The authorities gave us stern warnings. We heard that guardsmen had even killed four students, shot them to death in the grass. At first we were convinced that they were four students there in Washington, in our group. Everywhere we went, we wondered whether we should even be there at all.

We were on the grass near the Washington Monument, just waiting, when we became aware of some sort of disturbance on the hillside below us. Suddenly something burned my eyes, my sinuses. I thought something was terribly wrong with my face. It quickly got worse. I was dizzy, convinced the front of my head would explode. "Tear gas!" someone shouted. "Get them back on the bus!"

I noticed several other students weeping—a strange sight, strange to see all your friends crying all of a sudden.

But I was there, that was the important thing. I was wearing an orange bandoleer and a paper hat. I was a safety-patrol kid on the annual Washington Trip.

I never heard where the tear gas came from. The chaperones whispered among one another, looked out the window as we drove away, but didn't say much about it. They just said the Washington Monument was now *off*. One excursion after another was X'd off the schedule we'd memorized. After that teargas incident, all we got to see was away from the city, the Zoo, Mount Vernon. We didn't know that it was one of Washington's weirdest months on record.

On our unavoidable encounters with them, the hippies looked right through us. To the hippies, everyone else in Washington had an identity—especially their enemies. The hippies were there mainly to get the attention of those over 30, members of the Establishment. Those between 16 and 30, of course, were allies or potential allies. A few of them had babies, and they seemed to care for them. But to hippies, I thought, nothing could be more thoroughly irrelevant than an 11-year-old boy.

And, to be honest, they didn't mean much to us, either. To us, the hippies were mainly the people who ruined the Beatles. We had nothing against the war. We were as fond of war as all 11-year-old boys are. They were showing blood in the movies now, and we were all for it, cheered to see people blown apart in *Patton* and *Tora! Tora! Tora!*. We bought cap guns at the motel's souvenir store, especially loud metal pistols with hammer action, and speculated that we could convert them into real pistols if we just took that little bar out of the barrel. Through the bus windows on Pennsylvania Avenue, we banged away at hippies and soldiers both.

Horror sets in only later, with maturity. Still, even when we were eleven, we never played "Vietnam."

On a dare my friend Jimmy and I were going to take the stairs in the Washington Monument and race to the top, but after that tear gas thing they didn't take us back there at all. We'd all bragged about what we were going to see first at the Smithsonian, the *Spirit of St. Louis*, the Mercury capsule—but in the end we didn't get to see anything.

We spent the week at the hotel, loitering around the parking lot, watching trains go by in the back. Somewhere, one kid procured a big, ugly wad of some leafy substance. Looking back, I suspect it was chewing tobacco, but some of us smoked it in these hillbilly corncob pipes they had at that souvenir store. The afternoon when we were scheduled to be at the Smithsonian, an older kid began acting very strangely, and something in his room caught on fire. The arrival of overworked firemen that day was a small consolation.

Bored senseless and proud to be Tennesseans, my friends and I bought hokey hillbilly straw hats with felt patches to go with our corncob pipes, and chased each other through the hotel's suites barefoot, shooting each other with cap guns, once upsetting a formal banquet. I can only guess what a dozen armed 11-year-old hillbillies seem like to elegant Washingtonians in black tie—barefoot junior Tennesseans smoking corncob pipes and chasing each other around white-linened tables—but I remember that bold moment of civil disobedience as my own Demonstration, my contribution to the Counterculture.

Now my son's in Washington for his own safety-patrol trip. A lot of things have changed in 26 years. Nowadays they don't post safety-patrol kids several blocks away from the school, license them to stop traffic and let them tell little kids when they're allowed to cross—largely, I'm sure, because kids don't walk to school anymore. All safety-patrol kids do now is open car doors. The Washington buses they're using are air-conditioned, and they even have VCRs. And police escorts. And nowadays there probably aren't many people hurling tear gas around the Washington Monument.

Somehow, though, there's some continuity. This week, after all these years, this skinny kid who looks vaguely like me is finally getting his chance to see the *Spirit of St. Louis*.

—6/6/96

The Green Pavilion

Every morning that summer, I put on a bright-red shirt and dark polyester slacks and a nameplate that said JOHN. Then I left my back-door apartment and walked a block down the street to a gate where I showed a photo ID to a guard. At a fragrant old building inside the huge fence, I punched a time clock. Then about a dozen of us, all wearing identical bright-red shirts, would wait for our orders with a kind of giddy dread. It was the World's Fair, and we were crowd control.

Our assignments came: China Line. Egypt and Peru. Korean Dancers. Australia. Japan.

The China Line was the meanest. We tried several tactics to tame it, but nothing worked. At 10:30 the line was often more than 3,000 people long. It was our job to police it, keep it straight, keep people from breaking, bust up fights in the blazing heat.

Korea was madness too. You had to get there immediately if you wanted to see the Korean dancers. Because we spoke English and most of the Koreans didn't, it was often our job to talk to people who'd driven in from Wisconsin just to see the Korean dancers: mainly, to tell them that they wouldn't get to see the Korean dancers, not this trip.

Japan was tough in the morning. But in the afternoon, Japan was bliss. Better prepared than most of the mega-pavilions were, the Japanese tried to organize the daily disorder on the pavement outside their door, posting unflappable hostesses who could disarm the ugliest American.

Nearby, the modest European pavilions who took that energy/technology theme literally didn't draw the hordes that the Peruvian mummy and the Chinese statues did. They were so quiet that Erno Rubik, the shy inventor of the Rubik's Cube, then an international sensation, would sit out on the curb in front of the Hungary Pavilion unrecognized except by an occasional 9-year-old disciple who'd coax him into demonstrating, one more time, the Secret of the thing.

But mostly what made it so pleasant there was a tree: the huge elm that gave a green hush to the area. I don't remember any fights there, no heat strokes, no crowd-control emergencies.

Fifteen years ago, Fair planners recognized the usefulness of this sheltering elm and preserved it, building a rustic amphitheater around its base. Several times a day at the Elm Tree Theater, a band of loony troubadours would act out any story proposed by the audience, usually dominated by kids eating Belgian waffles. When Japan wasn't a problem, and it rarely was in the afternoon, I'd stand in the back and watch, and forget I was getting four bucks an hour to do this.

I'd spent so many full days on the blistering pavement that by July my hair was bleached a wheaty white and my skin had been kilned to the color of red-mud clay. I was a photographic negative of myself. In 20 years, I'm sure, I'll have a crop of souvenir World's Fair skin cancer. But for few hours on hot afternoons, that tree offered rare relief.

After the fair, the tree survived as everything around it changed. All the pavilions were demolished; the hillside was made almost unrecognizable by new landscaping; the Knoxville Museum of Art was built adjacent to it, about where Japan used to be. They built a courtyard around the tree itself, as if it were a carefully guarded exhibit. They named the museum's restaurant after that big tree you could see through the north window.

But last week the elm tree was gone. Cortese's tree surgeons finally admitted that it was too weak to survive a strong blow, and cut it down. Jim Cortese hoped an imaginative wood sculptor would shape some symbolic totem from the main trunk to display in the planned sculpture garden on the site—but so far that's just his dream.

What's there now is a table-sized stump with nearly a century's worth of rings. When it sprouted, along the shore of what some still called Scuffletown Creek, it was on the border between Knoxville's toniest neighborhood and a railroad/industrial section of foundries and glass factories and machine shops. The tree was there when the L&N first opened its fancy turn-of-the-century passenger terminal nearby—and still there 60 years later when the station closed down forever.

And it was there when hundreds of kids laughed at silly grownups doing wacky versions of "Goldilocks and the Three Bears."

Now it's gone, as everything must be sooner or later. But if I and my skin last a little longer than we might have otherwise, we might have that tree to thank.

—2/8/96

The Secret History Workout

One of the chief obstacles that people who study history have to deal with are prejudices that historians are overweight, underdeveloped, pasty-faced, nearsighted folk who never get any exercise.

Actually, scholars in several disciplines have to deal with that stereotype, but it's a special problem for historians. Because exercise has little historical context, to us it's really, really boring. Try to research "Exercise Routines of the Whigs," and you're liable to be frustrated. Our ancestors got plenty of exercise, no question. They just didn't do much of it on purpose. And they didn't call it "working out." They had quaint names for it like "walking to work," "hoeing the field," "beating the rugs."

Since then, alert, progressive-minded innovators have come up with labor-saving devices for us to buy, like automobiles and power mowers and remote controls. People bought these things, grateful for the new freedom not to exercise, and lost their muscle tone. Then, of course, more alert, progressive-minded innovators noted the health problems their popular labor-saving devices were causing by taking away our opportunities for exercise, so they came up with labor-provoking devices for us to buy, like workout tapes and exercycles and streamlined weight machines. It was just like old-fashioned work, except it didn't actually produce anything. It made plenty of sense, especially to the folks who sell all that stuff.

Anyway, that's my Short History of Exercise. But we still have the historian's problem. Much of the work historians do is what the cardiologists and proctologists call *sedentary* work, stuff you do mainly when you're sitting down. Obviously, what we have to do is work a little physical fitness into the research routine.

Fortunately, Knoxville is blessed with great historical workouts.

• To begin with, we're fortunate that our best resources are high up. The McClung Collection is on the third floor of the Customs House, up 58 stairs from the ground floor. Lawson McGhee's stacks, all their old magazines and microfilms of newspapers, are 43 steps up. The UT library's most interesting textbooks tend to be even loftier, up on the fifth and sixth floors.

All these places are served by elevators—the McClung Collection even has an old-fashioned cage-style historical elevator—but take the stairs, even if you're not as claustrophobic as I am. I've never even seen the inside of any Knoxville library's elevators, partly because I need the exercise and partly because seeing those doors close always makes me scream and climb on top of strangers. Like other local historians, I recall the fate of poor Edward Krutch, the only Krutch who ever tried to live an ordinary, respectable, low-profile life—but then died a horribly public death in one of Knoxville's first elevators.

So take the stairs. You might be breathing hard as you sign in at the McClung Collection, but remember that the blood coursing through your legs and heart is also coursing through your skull, bringing you new thoughts—along with all those important nutrients. Now you're thinking the active, healthy way.

• Don't sit down unless you have to. Lots of research can be done standing up. Sitting down is a commitment to a book or stack of books that may not turn out to be any good. Because you pull a book out and sit down with it, you may feel obliged to take it seriously and find some use for it, much like you would with a bad date. That can lead to bad history. Instead, play the field. That usually means standing up in the aisleway,

JACK NEELY

not sitting. You may get a crick in your shoulder, but it's much better for your cardiovascular system, your colon, and your historical perspective.

• Facing a choice between a slim volume and a weighty tome, take the latter. Some books tip the scale at 30 pounds or so, similar to some of those weights you can buy. At the library, weightlifting is free; you don't even have to pay to use the equipment. I especially recommend city directory research; each volume weighs 10 pounds or more. If you're researching the history of a 90-year-old house, say, you have to look at 90 of them. That's a half-ton of lifting, and it'll do you good.

• In some cities the microfiche viewers are motorized. But I'm grateful that here in Knoxville most of the publicly accessible machines are older models—DeSotos, I believe—with the hand crank on the right side. In my experience, if you're trying to find a particular date—say, July 20, 1969—it'll be at the very end of a very big roll labeled "October 12, 1492-July 20, 1969." You'll crank 100 repetitions, check the date, and repeat the first two steps as often as it takes. Feel the burn. Then, when you're done, you reverse it and crank an equal number of rotations backwards, bringing a slightly different group of muscles into play. They even have a setting where you can crank at a slower speed, giving you more exercise for less result—obviously an innovation for advanced microfiche enthusiasts unsatisfied with the crankage they get on the high setting. Either way, it's a great rotary arm exercise that works on both your biceps and triceps.

The only drawback is that it works only for the biceps and triceps on your right side. If you notice that some historians look especially burly on one side, that's the reason. Here's a tip: You can compensate, as you're cranking, by extending your left arm and making little circles in the air. Ignore the stares. Who do they think they are, anyway? Just remember that you're the healthiest historian in the room.

• Don't be lazy. Know that a good historian has to check absolutely everything, and the sooner the better, while it's fresh on your mind. If you see an address referred to in a story or an ad, drop everything and go out and look at the site. You won't understand what you're reading about until you do. Every time you see an address and can't recall what's there now, leave your source on the table and run downstairs, out the door, and down the street to have a look. You can usually be back in the library before they've even missed you. And if the librarians remark that you look healthy for a historian, it's because you've just had a historically aerobic workout.

Readers often ask me what I do when an idea for a column doesn't pan out. This is my solution this week.

—7/11/96

Ruminations From a
Union Avenue sidewalk

We knew it was somewhere inside there all these years, but as the mirrored glass comes off the old Miller's Building, people stop on Union Avenue and stare, as if they didn't expect to actually see it again, this sudden image of that huge dark-brick building with the tall arched windows. In spite of all the old photographs of it all around town, we'd forgotten it, and how huge it was. It seems for all the world like a new archaeological discovery, a battered temple emerging from some modernist jungle.

The last time I saw that wall, I was just a kid. When I was 12 or 13 and had a free Saturday because my clients' grass wasn't growing much, I'd get on the bus in front of my house. On Gay Street, near Union, I'd pull the cord and get out. Downtown was freedom to a pre-driving kid, the only place I could come and go as I pleased.

I had a regular circuit. I'd make a pass through Kress's 5 & 10. I'd also go by the Hobby Shop, which was next door to a bar and cigar shop on Clinch, and look at some model airplanes and monsters.

And I'd go to Wall Avenue. There, among the loan sharks and cheap jewelers and the Blue Circle, was a rare-coin shop. The proprietor was an old bald man with a long nose. He was rarely in a good mood, but he let me gawk at the Morgan dollars, liberty dimes, Indian pennies in his glass cases. I just looked, mostly, but sometimes I bought something cheap.

Once I bought an 1867 nickel at his shop for a half-dollar, then got tired of it and took it back in a fresh cellophane sleeve. He said he wouldn't buy it because it was no good.

He didn't like me a bit. Once he sold me some tiny gold coins dated 1853 for about five bucks. After a few humid weeks of summer, one of the gold coins developed a bubble. It popped, and I saw it was all rust inside. He wouldn't buy that back, either.

I thought of him as a mean, crabby, dishonest old man, but I'd go in his shop every chance I got.

And I went to Miller's. I didn't go much to that modern Miller's down on Henley; there was something about that place I didn't like; somehow it reminded me of a hospital or an airport. When I remember it I mainly remember standing around waiting for somebody.

I favored the one on Gay Street. I don't recall much about what they sold. Most of the floors, as I recall, featured rows and rows and rows and rows of cloth of one sort or another and didn't interest me. I don't remember ever buying anything at Miller's except for Hardy Boys books, which were on the mezzanine. The mezzanine was different, like a bazaar. I'd lean over and look at the shoppers on the first floor, who never looked up. A mezzanine lets a 12-year-old boy feel subversive, think about water balloons.

They had a small but always fresh selection of Hardy Boys books, seemingly a different combination of the blue hardbacks every time, and usually one or two I'd never seen. I always wanted the original editions from the '20s and '30s, which I thought were better than the ones after 1950. I'd buy them for $1.50, a couple hours' worth of work on a good day. I ended up getting all 50, and nearly all the ones I bought myself I got on the Miller's mezzanine.

Downstairs in the basement there was a little diner, and it was my favorite place to eat downtown. The S&W was too popular for me, a place you went with your family and in a mood to talk loudly. With so many people, I always felt self-conscious in the cafeteria line there. Just walking in there was like entering a beauty pageant. On the other hand, I wasn't quite bold enough for the storefront sandwich shops on Market Square and up and down Gay, the dark little places that served beer.

The Miller's Grill always suited my mood perfectly. I'd say it reminded me of Hopper's *Nighthawks*—but the truth is, the first time I saw Hopper's *Nighthawks* it reminded me of the Miller's Grill, except the place in the painting looked a little more cheerful than Miller's Grill because at least it had a nice big window to the outside. Since it was a grill, I always got the grilled cheese, because I figured that must be the specialty. I don't know why I liked sitting there at the counter by myself, drinking a Coke and eating a grilled cheese, but I did. It was what I always looked forward to, my reward for a successful day of shopping for a Hardy Boys book or an old nickel. I'd sit there and read the first two or three chapters; my favorite part was always the interesting characters the boys met at the beginning. Then I'd pull myself away barely in time to run up to Gay Street and catch the next bus home.

I suspect Hardy Boys books had a lot to do with why I liked downtown so much. Only downtown did I get to see the sorts of characters Franklin W. Dixon wrote about: hunchbacks, shoeshine boys, blind beggars, priests, loan sharks, hoboes, foreigners, reporters, grouchy old coin collectors, tough guys who looked like maybe they were as "swarthy" as the tough guys in Hardy Boys books always were. Those folks seemed scarce at the Racquet Club and the Burger Chef. But downtown always promised some adventure around the corner, over that transom, down that alley, up on that mezzanine.

It's something, seeing those old walls again for the first time in 25 years.

—9/24/98

JACK NEELY

CHAPTER SEVEN

SECRET SHRINES

A Live Birth

During the REM show at Thompson-Boling Arena earlier this month, the singer for the most popular rock 'n' roll band in the world stopped the performance to read from James Agee's "Knoxville: Summer 1915." The Knoxville audience didn't seem to get it at first, hooting as if they were still playing "Crush With Eyeliner." Michael Stipe insisted that they listen, implied that this was one reason he was looking forward to playing Knoxville, that they should feel proud to live in a city that raised James Agee. He started over.

Suddenly respectful—or intimidated—8,000 rock 'n' roll fans shut up and listened. But some in the crowd had obviously never heard of the guy.

Obviously there's a whole new crop of freshmen who missed my column about Agee back in May. People used to kid me about my preoccupation with Agee, and I've sometimes wondered if one can over-revere a guy who was, after all, just a mortal human organism like the rest of us. The thing about Agee was that he somehow described the human condition, came closer than anyone I know in his effort to "tell the sorrow of being on this earth," using a language that wasn't designed for that sort of business.

James Agee's birthday is coming up on Monday the 27th. In some cities the birthdays of lesser souls are celebrated with readings and festivals. I don't expect we ever will celebrate Agee's, unless we can designate it James Agee Christmas Bargain Day.

Of course, we've discreetly erased most traces of his life here. The old Highland Avenue address he wrote about is now an apartment building. The site of the old Majestic Theater is now the blank side of a bank. His Asylum Avenue Viaduct is now an unnoticeable interstate connection. But when I lived in Fort Sanders in the '70s, I kept hearing rumors that one building remained: James Agee's actual birthplace.

A few years ago, a friend told me she'd seen Agee's birth certificate, and the birthplace listed was not his home on Highland, but a residence on Clinch Avenue. She told me she'd misplaced her copy. Another likely source didn't have it, either. Then I was told it was on file somewhere in Nashville and that legally it wouldn't be a public record until 2009.

But months later, my friend surprised me in the office with a photo-copy: a Knoxville Board of Health birth certificate of the son of a post office employee, one James Rufus Agee. The address on the certificate was 1115 West Clinch.

I dropped what I was doing and walked out of the building and across the Clinch viaduct. There, where 1115 is supposed to be, is a big squat of upscale condos. I'd become aware of them about 10 years ago, when the people who lived there would complain to the police about the blues my friends played on the porch across 11th. *If they don't like the blues*, we wondered, *why did they move into Fort Sanders?* We always regarded them curiously but didn't get too close.

Back at the McClung Collection, I looked up the address in old city directories and found that 1115 Clinch was the address of James Agee's maternal grandparents, the Tylers. Their house was on the corner of Clinch and 12th. Agee's 25-year-old mother apparently felt more com-fortable about having her first baby at her own mom's house, several blocks away from her husband's.

Years later, when his mom was acting nutty, the teenage Agee actually moved in with his grandparents on Clinch for more than a year, during which time he attended Knoxville High, which he'd soon be lampooning in some of his first fiction.

His grandparents and his Uncle Hugh, the artist, left that house soon afterward, and the Tyler house became the longtime home of a local grocer. By the '50s the Tylers' old house was split into five apartments.

Part of the rumor I'd heard long ago turned out to be true. The Agee Birthplace actually did survive the more famous Agee home on Highland. A couple of married students named Harmon were living there in the late '60s. The house stood vacant for a time. Then, around 1970, it was torn down.

You can make too much of a birthplace. I've never seen my own birthplace, which is (or was) a military clinic in northern Japan. I don't have any strong desire to see it. But for some reason, I would have liked to see Agee's.

If it were still here, Michael Stipe and other pilgrims would at least have something to come look at.

—11/22/95

The Horrid Slaughter

Toward the end of the 1982 World's Fair, I wanted a job as a tour guide in the museum of Egyptian archaeology. It sounded like better work than another job somebody thought would be perfect for me, poring over receipts in a windowless office on Cedar Bluff, failing to sort out the World's Fair housing mess. To prove I was perfect for a transfer, I borrowed all the library's books about Egyptian history and mythology, with special attention to the reign of Queen Hatshepsut and the artifacts on display in the pavilion. I got the job. So for six weeks, in a blazer and khakis, I passed for an Egyptologist.

The most striking thing about studying this foreign 5,000-year-old civilization where they worshipped dung beetles and mummified cats was how *familiar* these stories were. There was one story about a prince who suspects his uncle of having assassinated his father, the king, and with the help of his mother and his father's ghost, defeats him.

The story of the Egyptian deity Horus is the story of Hamlet. I began to understand that people die, nations die, languages die—but stories don't die. Stories survive the centuries, just with different characters playing the leading roles.

Hollywood's latest corruption of an old story is called *Anastasia*, made as if on a dare from someone who didn't believe you could use the Russian Revolution and the massacre of the Romanovs as the premise for a cartoon with cute animals. A large family slaughtered, a child secretly spared who lives among us in disguise. The Russians didn't invent that story. I doubt the Knoxvillians did either—but ours is much older.

In West Knoxville historical allusions are rare. Given the chance to name streets, most developers opt for the titles of make-believe British earls. But on one corner in the modern subdivision West Hills, a short street called Doublehead Lane *T*'s into a longer street called Alexander Cavet Drive. In 1793, very near this quiet suburban intersection, the Doublehead of Doublehead Lane murdered Alexander Cavet and his family. Nearby, a stone marker over what's believed to be a mass grave tells a small part of the story.

If we can believe the white man's histories, Doublehead was the most ruthless of all Cherokee chiefs. Leader of the rebellious anti-white band the Chickamaugans, Doublehead didn't get along with many of his own people. To call him a bloodthirsty savage is too accurate to be politically incorrect. Doublehead had reportedly cooked and eaten some victims. Many of the Cherokee feared and hated Doublehead, called him Kill-Baby.

Doublehead led a band of perhaps 1,000 Indians, mostly Creeks and Cherokees, who sought vengeance against the white nation they may have suspected could never be kept within boundaries by peaceful means. The actions of the pan-tribal Chickamaugans weren't sanctioned by the Cherokee rank and file, who were still betting they could trust the white man. Most Cherokees found the Chickamaugans' methods too vicious and their goal—to drive all whites back east of the Appalachians—unrealistic.

Doublehead and the others approached Knoxville—the capital of the white Southwestern Territory in 1793—with the intention of destroying it once and for all. At no other time in history—including the federal artillery assault, the Confederate artillery assault, or the entire Cold War—did Knoxville come so close to being obliterated.

But an argument between the two chiefs, Doublehead and John Watts, stalled them out some eight miles west of town. Reportedly, one point of contention was whether to kill all the men in Knoxville—or all the men, women, *and* children. While they debated, Knoxville's tiny garrison executed a diversionary tactic as Sevier's army approached from the distant south.

Frustrated by their confusion about where Knoxville's defenders were, the Chickamaugans besieged a tiny fort called Cavet's Station, manned by three armed men and 10 women and children. In the battle the Cavets killed two Indians and wounded three others before an English-speaking

Chickamaugan offered generous terms of surrender: The whites were to be taken captive and traded for Indian captives.

But as soon as the white men emerged, Doublehead and a few allies rushed in and killed them. Then they murdered the other 10 members of the Cavet family, scalped and/or disemboweled them, and strewed body parts across the shrubs and gardens of Cavet Station. They burned the fort to the ground.

"Not one," reported the *Knoxville Gazette*, "escaped the horrid carnage."

At least that's how the original reports had it. Within a few months, a story surfaced that one of Cavet's children was spared when John Watts, another Cherokee leader, interrupted Doublehead's orgy of slaughter.

A recent PBS documentary about Anastasia questioned the Russian myth, quoting experts about how rare mercy is among mass killers. Maybe, scholars speculate, it's because the massacre of an entire family is so horrible to contemplate that we come up with these stories of a lone survivor, an innocent child. But maybe it's because sometimes it actually happens that way.

For years there were rumors that one young Cavet had survived. By most accounts, the survivor was a boy, the youngest member of the Cavet family.

But there are as many stories as there are tellers. By one, the child-survivor was a baby boy who "soon began screaming so much he was bashed against a tree and killed." One letter from South Carolina in 1794 reported the child was living among the Creeks. Thomas Humes, in the address he gave on the occasion of Knoxville's 50th birthday, in 1842, outlined the Cavet tragedy and mentioned a child "saved by John Watts, taken as prisoner to the Creek Nation, and afterward tomahawked."

But by a couple of stories, the child who was saved was a girl. One report has the Cavet survivor as an 8-year-old girl named *Nacie*—an unusual name then and now. It sounds like a diminutive. It could almost be an American nickname for Anastasia.

—1/15/98

Irish Town

Lots of folks will tell you they're Irish. Given a couple pints of Guinness, I will, too. But most Southerners with vaguely Irish names are *Scots*-Irish, which means we're descendants of Scottish clans who'd lived in Ireland for a few generations before crossing the ocean, which most of us did more than 200 years ago.

After a generation or two of living in the woods, we might as well have been from anywhere. We lost our accents. Irish became *Arsh*, a modifier for *taters*. When our Catholic cousins started showing up here around 1850, we probably cussed the brawling papists, puzzled by their accent, befuddled when they crowded the Lamar House to celebrate an old Catholic saint that we'd thoroughly forgotten.

There were suddenly hundreds of them here, immigrants fleeing the potato famine and seeking jobs and homes in the New World—the same big wave of Irish immigration that changed Boston, New York, Chicago.

What brought them to Knoxville was work on the new railroad. Many of them built houses within sight of the train station on the formerly swampy wasteland on the north side of town. Irish Town eventually comprised maybe a dozen city blocks wrapping around the station, much of it now sliced up by the interstate. Its cultural center was the small stone Catholic church built in 1855 on top of the steep hill above Irish Town.

Judging by old city directories, Irish Town reached its peak in the 1880s, when they built a much bigger church on that hill, with an Irish Catholic school adjacent. Many houses among the suddenly dense blocks contained more than one nuclear family. Along Jackson, Depot, Park (later Magnolia), and farther north, there were Donahoes, Sheas, Callahans, Harrigans, Fitzgeralds, Malones, Kavanaughs, Murphys, Gillespies, Kennedys, Donivans, Gallivans, McGuires.

There was always a liberal smattering of non-Irish in Irish Town—black residents throughout the unsegregated neighborhood, as well as other immigrants with names like Finkelstein and Lukouski and Karstaadt. But for a generation or two, the Irish dominated. You could wander for half a mile from the train station and never be out of earshot of the brogue.

Patrick Sullivan, a young immigrant from County Kerry, was one of the founders, perhaps the first to open a business in the area, a grocery on what was then called Crozier, now Central. In the 1880s he built the saloon that still operates under his name. Several Irish ran saloons, like John O'Byrne, whose bar was practically next door to Sullivan's. Callaghan's was around the corner on Depot. Curran's and McGuire's were nearby. Some were outside the physical parameters of Irish Town but Irish nonetheless: For years, "Red" Mike Cullinan ran a rough-edged place up on Market Square. Tom O'Connor's saloon on Cumberland doubled as a museum of unearthed curios.

At its height the Irish community could depend on itself for nearly everything: Irish groceries, Irish restaurants, Irish hardware. Some insisted that it should do so; Irish were expected to patronize Irish businesses exclusively. But the close community's power extended deep into mainstream Knoxville. Martin Condon, an Irish immigrant's son, became mayor of Knoxville in 1888 and apparently favored Catholic employees. One story holds that an Irish Catholic city plumbing inspector, hired by an Irish Catholic city official, lost his job when he married a non-Catholic.

By the turn of the century, the neighborhood was disintegrating. The portion of Central that was the original spine of Irish Town was now known as the Bowery, condemned by zealous reformers as the most dangerous avenue in the South outside of New Orleans. Irish saloons closed down, along with all the others, in 1907. The Catholic parish split, opening a new church several blocks north. Many Irish became wealthy and bought cars and moved to larger houses and yards. Even the Sullivans moved to the 'burbs, settling in the Fourth and Gill neighborhood. Irish Town dried up, desiccated by success.

John O'Connor was the classic Irish kid, born to a working-class family in Irish Town in 1881. He dropped out of school at 12, taught himself at night, carried newspapers and messages during the day, played baseball, boxed. Around Irish Town they called him "Punch."

A bold union leader who became mayor of Knoxville in the New Deal '30s, O'Connor may be most often cited as the Democrat who came closest to breaking the Republican death-grip on the Second Congressional District. Republican J. Will Taylor made much of Democrat O'Connor's Catholicism: elect O'Connor, Taylor said, and Pope Pius XI will have a representative in Congress.

Knoxville went overwhelmingly for native son O'Connor anyway. But the surrounding countryside, especially dyed-in-the-wool Republican Scott County, made the difference. Taylor got the job. To this day our Second District has not sent a Democrat to Congress since before the Civil War.

By 1936, when the voluble O'Connor ran for Congress, bragging about being born and raised in Old Irish Town, he sometimes had to explain what he was talking about.

—3/14/96

The Sacred Dust

In a cotton field near the Tallapoosa River deep in Alabama was a lone gravestone enclosed with a low wrought-iron fence. The stone had been there for decades, marking a grave that was even older. Months, sometimes years passed without anyone visiting the grave.

The June morning in 1889 when a large delegation arrived in carriages, cotton pickers in this remote field must have watched curiously. There were dozens of men, all in coats and ties. They stood around the grave and posed for a photograph. Two of them made speeches.

One was Alabama's Governor Seay. One was Dr. John Mason Boyd, perhaps the most esteemed physician in Knoxville, best known for gynecological surgery. Another was a professor from Auburn. The one with the jauntiest pose—leaning, feet crossed, something like Teddy Roosevelt with a bagged caribou—was the flamboyant young governor of Tennessee, Bob Taylor.

Then Richard DeArmond, the custodian of the Courthouse back in Knoxville, picked up a shovel, shoved it into the earth in front of the gravestone, and began to dig. Others helped. They weren't sure they'd find anything at all.

Hardly more than two feet down, the clay crumbled and fell into an oblong cavity. Not exactly rectangular, the cavity was an irregular hexagon, long and symmetrical, shaped exactly like an old-fashioned coffin: the kind of coffin that had gone out of style years ago, before the war, wider at the shoulders than at the feet. But within the hole there was no actual coffin. And, they noted with some disappointment, no skull. At first, it appeared there was nothing in the hole at all. But stirring around in the coffin-shaped cavity, they found two bones, one six inches, the other eight inches long. The doctors agreed they must be thigh bones. Then they found several teeth, small white particles, and traces of a substance the doctors called "disintegrated animal matter." And exactly 12 hand-made nails. They scooped it all up and put it in a casket and drove back to Montgomery. They handled it with care because what they had in the casket was all that was left of John Sevier.

He'd died near that spot 74 years earlier, on a surveying expedition just after the War of 1812. A rampant fever that had already killed several younger soldiers did the old man in. Survivors buried him hastily, marking his grave only with a charred log from the campfire.

The grave was nearly forgotten; back in Tennessee, we often regretted that our first governor's burial site was unknown. But there was always at least one person who knew where it was; for decades, that person was an Alabama neighbor named Littleberry Strange.

See, in the summer of 1834, Strange had encountered a man named John Harbison who said he'd helped bury Sevier. He recalled the spot, told Strange he'd marked it with that partially burned oak log. Along with Captain William Walker, a Sevier protégé, they poked around until they found it, a two-and-a-half-foot fragment of the oak marker that hadn't rotted away in 19 years. Captain Walker marked it again with a "lightwood knot," intending to return and build a grand monument to his hero. But Captain Walker was mortal, too; he died three years later, as did the younger Harbison. Perhaps oppressed with the weight of being the only mortal who knew about the unmarked grave of a hero, Strange replaced the knot with a modest marble tombstone.

Through the decades, including two wars, Strange quietly tended John Sevier's grave, eventually installing a little wrought-iron fence around it.

It wasn't until years after the Civil War that rumors about the grave made the rounds in Nashville. During Bob Taylor's administration in the late 1880s, it was determined that the hero of Tennessee should be exhumed and reburied in his home state. And what better spot than the lawn of the new courthouse in Knoxville?

The exhumation party placed John Sevier's remains—the Sacred Dust, they called it—inside a modern metallic rosewood-trimmed, silver-handled coffin, hand-made in Cincinnati and lined with "the most expensive French satin." Loaded on a train—an invention Sevier never saw in his lifetime— it made the 300-mile trip to Knoxville. A huge military parade carried the coffin all the way down Gay Street from the train station to the courthouse. Marching alongside the coffin were companies of Union and Confederate veterans, Catholic Knights, the German and Irish immigrants' fraternities, the Oddfellows, marching bands—the marshal of each company in black coats, black leggings, black slouch hats, and a red sash.

Massed around the three-year-old courthouse in every direction on that afternoon of June 19 was a crowd of 20,000, but they say only 10,000 were standing close enough to hear the eulogies. Among them were several distinguished visitors: Governor Seay of Alabama; Adolph Ochs, the young editor from Chattanooga, returning to his childhood home for this remarkable occasion. The official orators were Governor Taylor, perhaps the most popular speaker in the South in 1889; Thomas Humes, the Episcopal rector and elderly former president of UT; Col. William Harrison, the railroad lawyer; Captain J.R. McCallum, the poet; and Presbyterian minister James Park. These stalwarts spoke about Governor Sevier for more than three hours into the cool of the June evening. None of them knew John Sevier, of course. His body had been buried in Alabama longer than he had been alive.

They'd exhume the governor again, four years later, to build a large obelisk in his memory. They'd store his casket in the courthouse and regret that it had already suffered water damage.

Today the 20,000 who witnessed John Sevier's reburial are buried, too. Still, we're pretty sure that that is indeed his true grave, beneath the great monument on the lawn. Though there may not be much of him left but the silver handles of his second casket and, perhaps, a few nails.

—6/18/98

The Knoxvilles That Never Were

One century ago this Monday, Knoxville's annual Street Fair and Carnival was in full swing, drawing 15,000 to 40,000 attendees daily to witness spectacles like Buffalo Bill's Wild West Show, starring seven buffalo, 580 horses, and 600 performers, including 60 Indians and, of course, Bill himself.

But the four-day festival's single most anticipated event was on the Courthouse lawn, where "a great mass of sandwiched humanity" crowded around an elaborately decorated platform. That morning saw three speakers: young Knoxville lawyer and future U.S. Supreme Court Justice Edward Terry Sanford; a mysterious ceremonial figure known as The Prophet of the Great Smokies, represented as a white-bearded Neptune with horns; and one bald middle-aged man with a handlebar mustache, the speaker these thousands really came to see.

His name was Robert Taylor, and he was the thrice-elected governor of Tennessee; we called him "Our Bob." The subject of his speech was Knoxville as it would be in the year 1997.

"I almost wish I could live through the coming century to witness the triumphs which await," he declared. "This great valley of East Tennessee will be a glittering chain of cities and splendid towns for 250 miles, and the sky at night will be red with the reflection of light from her furnaces and factories, and she will be the center of population and the richest country in the world. She will sit on her 700 hills, and Knoxville will be the hub of her glory. Gay Street will reach from Clinton to Maryville. The University of Tennessee will be the greatest institution of learning on the continent, and there will be a carnival every day…except the holy Sabbath."

He went on to declare that in 1997 the *Knoxville Daily Tribune* would have a circulation of one million. And if all that wasn't incredible enough, he predicted, "the women will vote…."

Taylor's predictions probably seemed perfectly believable to those who stood listening that October morning. The 1890s, following the landmark Chicago Exposition of 1893, was a credulous decade: the City Beautiful era, when American cities tried to seem as impressive as Paris and the greatest European cities.

For more than two centuries, the Upper Tennessee Valley has been a sort of twilight zone in American history, a gloaming that's been conducive to dreams. Though the Knoxville area was "settled" relatively early in American history and is central to the oldest and still most populous third of the nation, the mountains and dense forests have kept much of it remote and undeveloped all those years. With its green hills and clean-looking rivers, abundant wildlife and vegetation, East Tennessee can still seem like a paradise. Its myths and mounded relics still breed visions, based more on imagination than evidence, of ancient civilizations and peaceful peoples living in harmony with nature and each other. It was, and remains, exactly the sort of place that gives Utopians big ideas.

Maybe it shouldn't be so surprising that this area has been central to several Utopian projects over the decades.

Way back in 1736, a German idealist named Christian Gottlieb Priber lived among the Cherokee at Tellico and attempted to found a Kingdom of Paradise, where people of all races would share possessions and children alike. Priber's proto-communist state apparently sounded fine to the Cherokee, but the British colonial authorities had him jailed for subversive dreaming.

Over a century later, Swiss tailor Peter Staub became involved with a Swiss company that bought 20 square miles in Grundy County, about 100 miles southwest of Knoxville. Staub touted the community, to be called Gruetli, as a sylvan all-Swiss paradise, attracting about 300 Swiss immigrants to the settlement. But most of the innocents were disappointed with the extreme conditions in the mountains. Years later the survivors of Gruetli called Staub a "first-class swindler."

Perhaps chastened, Staub chose to found an architectural paradise—a European-style opera house—on Gay Street. Staub's Theater was the region's standard for entertainment for decades. Swindler or not, we liked Staub. We elected him mayor of Knoxville twice.

East Tennessee's most famous utopia, of course, came still later. English author Thomas Hughes scouted the U.S. to find a "New Jerusalem" where unlanded gentry could make their own destinies, earning an honest living through manual labor, forming a model city for the corrupt world beyond. In 1880 Hughes began building Rugby, named after his old prep school, some 50 miles northwest of Knoxville, a place where civilized people would live in peace and harmony like nowhere else.

Before that idealistic decade was over, another British-born dreamer, Alexander Arthur—a lumber magnate who actually lived in Knoxville—was planning another paradise, Middlesborough, Kentucky. His new town at Cumberland Gap would become one of America's industrial capitals and a playground for the world elite.

By the time Taylor spoke at Knoxville's courthouse lawn, Rugby was already failing, and although Arthur's extravagant Four Seasons Hotel had attracted royalty, it was clear that Middlesboro—spelled without Arthur's prefered *ugh*—would never be the citadel the dreamer envisioned.

We've known dozens of other dreamers over the years, like another Swiss-born Knoxvillian, Albert Chavannes of East Fourth Avenue. His 1895 novel, *In Brighter Climes*, posited a "perfect" civilization without religion or marriage in an African nation called Socioland. It was set in the distant future of 1950.

Other utopians have focused their fantasies on Knoxville proper.

Palmyra

Dr. Nicholas Romayne was a controversial New York doctor and med-school professor whose battles with Columbia University, of which he was a trustee, were legendary. "He was a strange, interesting man," goes one description in a bicentennial history of Columbia: "erudite but emotional, calculating but rash, enormous but indefatigable, a 300-pound phenomenon with a light, precise step."

Romayne was also a close business associate of territorial Governor William Blount, the man who had put the capital here and owned much of the land hereabouts. In 1795 the paradoxical Romayne was looking south, to the four-year-old territorial capital known as Knoxville, to establish a New World paradise. It's unclear whether Dr. Romayne ever spent much time here, but something convinced him that a new city in the area could be marketed as a haven for European immigrants.

Most of what we know about Romayne's dream comes from a letter Blount wrote on April 20, 1795, to his brother John in North Carolina. He describes Romayne's remarkable plan to "lay out a large city, two miles square," well over 1,000 acres, adjacent to Knoxville.

"This great city is to be called Palmyra and to be laid out upon some new and elegant plan and to be handsomely delineated," wrote Governor Blount to his brother.

Blount had named Knoxville. Romayne apparently came up with the more graceful *Palmyra*. That ancient Greek city, an oasis of sculptures and mosaics in the Syrian desert, was described in a popular 1753 survey called *The Ruins of Palmyra*. For decades, idealistic communities called Palmyra sprang up across America.

"But all this to yourself," Blount warned his brother, "for profound Secrecey [sic] is essential… for as yet I have not purchased all the Land for this City…."

Fully occupied, Palmyra's 6,000 one-fifth-acre lots would have been one of America's larger cities in 1795. Romayne expected to clear a net profit of $80,000—in 1795 dollars. "It's a Scheme that may afford Profits to us without the possibility of a Loss," wrote Blount.

Romayne tailored the plan to attract buyer-residents from Europe, a land-buying market Blount had been trying to crack for years. John Chisholm, Scottish tavernkeeper and Blount's next-door neighbor and sidekick, was to do a lot of the footwork on the project.

Unfortunately for historians, their "Secrecey" was a little too profound. References to Palmyra drop out of the Blounts' correspondence after 1795. We don't know why, but it's easy to speculate.

Blount was soon preoccupied with founding a new state. Then, in 1797, Blount, Romayne, and Chisholm alike were in big trouble for another, even bigger Scheme. Together they masterminded a complex plot, not fully understood to this day, to forcefully colonize Spanish Louisiana and Florida for the British. By some accounts, Blount would be British governor of Louisiana in New Orleans while Romayne would reign over Natchez. How Palmyra might have folded into their plan for a British Louisiana is not recorded.

The tangled web remembered by historians as the Blount Conspiracy unraveled in 1797. Chisholm, serving the plot as a secret agent in England, was jailed there. Dr. Romayne was imprisoned in Philadelphia; upon his release in 1798, he exiled himself to Edinborough, where he became the first American professor at the Royal College of Physicians. Blount abdicated his U.S. Senate seat and remained a fugitive from justice for almost three years, until March 1800 when he collapsed suddenly at his Blount Mansion piazza and died.

Dr. Romayne returned to America after Blount's death and regained his reputation for both controversy and medical learning, founding the College of Physicians and Surgeons in New York.

We can only guess about exactly where the lost city of Palmyra was to be. Blount owned land all over, but since this two-square-mile spread was to be adjacent to original Knoxville, we might assume Palmyra's boundaries are entirely within today's city limits.

In Halls, right off Emory Road, is one short street called Palmyra Drive. But don't go there looking for utopian history. Palmyra Drive is the entrance to a modern residential neighborhood called Palmer Hills. It apparently has a palm-tree theme.

The Fountainhead

The springs north of town inspired utopians of fundamentalist tendencies; since before the Civil War, what was called the Fountainhead attracted evangelical camp meetings where Baptists would go to sleep in tents, roam in the woods, and listen to lots of reviving sermons.

In 1885, as the era of camp meetings faded, gilded-age speculators built a very different version of the resort. Designed like a millionaire's chateau, the Fountainhead Hotel was an elaborate luxury spot with 50 rooms across its three stories, an Italian band playing in the evenings, hot and cold running water on each floor.

One Kentucky visitor, a Colonel J.C. Woodward, was especially impressed—but he had even bigger ideas for it. He bought 431 acres around the hotel and built a heart-shaped pool at the springs. If the Fountainhead had lost its monastic simplicity, it retained a strain of revivalism about it.

Woodward moved here himself and marketed the Fountainhead area as a sort of Baptist utopia: "The new town will be a town where the saloon and whiskey grocery store will never be seen. We intend to make it a great educational center where the morals are as pure as the bracing atmosphere and the life-giving water."

In the early 1890s, the Fountainhead hosted band concerts, beauty contests, even hot-air balloon ascensions. The great Governor Bob Taylor gave rousing motivational speeches in the park. A new college, Holbrook Normal, opened up in an impressive new building nearby, enrolling more than 100 students.

But financial pressures—and a few unfortunate fires that destroyed both the old hotel and the college—amended Woodward's dream of a new town with pure morals. By the 20th century, the Fountainhead was beginning to resemble the more realistic—but still distinct—suburb we now know as Fountain City. There's not much Woodward-style utopian idealism left; but more than a century after the colonel envisioned his temperance paradise, Fountain City remains, in number of bars per capita, the driest section of Knoxville.

A Different Brownlow

The late 19th century was a dreamy era. The 20th century was a more practical one. What made the newer generation of utopians different from previous ones was meticulous planning. In 1913, Knoxville hosted the National Conservation Exposition—sometimes called the first "futuristic" fair in American history. It inspired some fairgoers with improbable dreams of a protected National Park in the Smokies timberland.

The next idyll came not from a revivalist or lone dreamer or land speculator; it came, at least indirectly, from the City Council and electorate of Knoxville. A referendum in March 1923 dumped the whole office of Knoxville mayor, opting for the city-manager form of municipal government shown to accomplish great things in some progressive cities. The man picked was Louis Brownlow, a Missouri-born, nationally famous genius of public administration. Louis Brownlow had been for years a globetrotting journalist who'd once been on the staff of *The Statesman of India*. He'd seen the great cities of the world but had no connection with Knoxville before 1923— except that he'd once served the *Knoxville Sentinel* as a Washington correspondent. (Son of a Confederate soldier, Brownlow was only a distant cousin of Knoxville's own firebrand Unionist and Reconstruction-era Governor "Parson" Brownlow.) Brownlow had become fascinated with public policy and had most recently been city manager of Petersburg, Virginia.

Here Brownlow hired out-of-state professionals to run the city and invent a new Knoxville. Besides untangling a considerable fiscal mess, he and his staff saw an acute need for beautification through urban sculpture, tree planting, public parks, and architectural standards; for a cohesive center of government downtown; and for a newfangled thing called zoning. Brownlow also introduced the idea of urban planning to a skeptical populace, made law of several of his plans, including zoning, and founded Knoxville's first City Planning Commission.

He also proposed a 16 percent tax hike to pay for it all.

To some Knoxvillians, that was the key part of his proposal. A reaction led by Councilman Lee Monday and his South Knoxville constituency branded Brownlow "King Louis I" and stalled his programs in City Council. Several of Brownlow's supporters on City Council were voted out of office.

Frustration with some conservative elements here left him with a headache that some whispered was a nervous breakdown. He quit in 1926, after less than three years on the job, and several members of his staff left with him. His spirit didn't leave, at least not right away; it re-emerged years after his physical departure.

Talahi

Perhaps inspired by Brownlow's efforts, one developer attempted to implement them, on a small scale, through the private sector.

Robert Foust was in his mid-40s, a competent planner with a conservative real-estate firm; he had dreams but, as yet, no outstandingly unusual accomplishments when he came up with an idea of establishing an idyllic planned community—a first for Knoxville—along the Tennessee River just west of town. Rather than just another residential subdivision, Talahi—Cherokee for "in the oaks"—would be a perfect community. Here, and only here, would people live in perfect accord with each other and with nature: "a natural loveliness adapted to a community life, often dreamed but seldom realized."

A student of Native American mythology, Foust sought to combine Cherokee symbols with English architecture and voguish Egyptian-influenced art-deco stylings in cast-stone monuments—a Panther Fountain and obelisk, a Sunhouse Fountain, a walled enclosure for small children called Papoose Park—to be the centerpieces and symbols of the new community.

He outlined his plan in a rhapsodic promotional book, with illustrations of a Tudor-style commercial center called Council Points. Strict rules mandated English-style architecture for all houses; natural features, hilly slopes, most trees, and even the neighborhood's distinctive stone outcroppings would be kept as close to their natural state as possible. "In TALAHI'S virgin forest," Foust's brochure read, "nature rules supreme. Its charm has not been subject to ruinous exploitation. On the contrary, the creators of this community have preserved for all time its natural beauty, adding to it only splendid adaptations of the landscape architect. Nothing has been done ruthlessly, not a tree has been disturbed nor a branch cut without forethought for the finished picture. Such is the setting of TALAHI—surpassed in natural charm by no other location in America...."

One passage in Foust's brochure sounds socialistic enough to give a good Republican the heebie-jeebies: "Greater beauty could remain in allowing each lot to conform to the natural contour of the ground.... Each lot remains a part of one vast park where one's neighbor's property becomes a part of one's own—a succession of home locations long dreamed of by men, but seldom found."

Foust insisted that "each home must necessarily improve and never detract from the development of the whole community.... Even business with its bustle must conform in Council Points to the touch of the artistic, to the grandeur of the forest..."

If Talahi was to be a shared-land commune, it was a commune strictly for the wealthy. In May 1929, lots went up for sale at $4,000 to $10,000, the steepest prices in Knoxville at the time.

Whether because of the price tag or skepticism about the new idea, it wasn't an instant success. Only one lot sold that summer. (Foust himself stayed put in his UT-area home.) That October came the Crash. The whole venture collapsed. Talahi was absorbed into a more conventional neighborhood called Sequoyah Hills.

In his Market Street office four years later, Foust shot himself. The cast-stone monuments that didn't succeed in attracting buyers in 1929 are now only appealing oddities along Cherokee Boulevard and Talahi, the street named for Foust's dream.

A City Plan

Meanwhile, even with Manager Brownlow long gone, some of the machines he'd set in motion kept churning out interesting proposals. In September 1929, his City Planning Commission signed an astonishing document: A Comprehensive City Plan for Knoxville.

With idealism, ambition, and confidence rarely seen since—plus striking photographs, fold-out maps, and stylish graphics—the Plan made the well-planned Knoxville of the Future look like a gleaming citadel. "Through the adequate treatment of its public building group," planners declared, "Knoxville may establish herself as the leader of the entire South in the expression of civic consciousness."

Still, the plan looked hard at Knoxville's shortcomings. Many of its recommendations are eerily prophetic:

• "The Tennessee River, which divides the city, is lined with picturesque bluffs rising on both sides of its course. Much of the waterfront is as yet unspoiled. The region is teeming with possibilities. Knoxville has but to develop the natural resources at hand to become an outstanding American city....Plans for the reclamation of this great asset to the city should be carried out...." Riverfront parks are suggested.

• Noting that without protective zoning, older neighborhoods central to the city were already losing their better-heeled residents who, "having lost confidence, start a panic like a run on a bank," moving to more distant subdivisions, the Plan scolded: "Expensive services of water, gas, electricity, sewers, and transportation are maintained at a greater cost in order to get...to the more distant and newly fashionable location. The total economic cost is enormous, and this loss and the risk of it are paid by the people...."

• "Billboards existing in many parts of the city are...extremely unattractive," the Plan warned. "The eventual elimination of these nuisances will add to property values and enhance the appearance of the city."

• "Certain parts of Knoxville present particularly barren and unattractive appearances because of the absence of trees bordering the streets. Tree planting should be carried on by the city in much the same manner as other street improvements."

• "In respect to parks, Knoxville might aptly be called, 'The city of neglected opportunities.' Considering...the city is unsurpassed for sheer natural beauty, the failure to take advantage of the existing assets is indeed surprising."

• "Considering the historical background of the city, Knoxville is greatly lacking in monuments....No cognizance has been taken of the intensely interesting persons and events that helped make the early history of Knoxville."

• "Too little attention has been paid in the past to proper setting of public buildings...."

• "A new city jail and municipal courts building is of pressing importance."

The text goes on to make its most astonishing proposal: a "Civic Center in City Hall Park." As described and drawn in 1929, it was to be a large, campus-style civic complex, five large buildings sprawling across four blocks in strikingly beautiful art-moderne architecture; the central building would have a tall, cathedral-like tower. Included would be separate city and county government buildings, a grassy park, an "Art and Historical Museum," and a "combined municipal and county jail and court" building. They didn't happen to use the phrase Justice Center.

"If such a plan is not followed," the text warned, "it is probable that fully as much or more money will be spent in purchasing sites and carrying out individual projects as expediency might direct, and the final results would be much less satisfactory."

The site recommended for the complex was an inexpensive 14-acre area bounded by Henley, Wall, Walnut, and old Vine; the original Main Street/riverfront site, they said, presented too many problems. But if the old Main Street courthouse site were kept, planners urged that the municipal center include "a terraced riverfront park between the public building group and the river."

In passing, the Plan also praised the new Talahi project. Both victims of the Depression, forgotten when the Depression was over. Some aspects of the Plan were put into effect, most notably the widening of Henley Street into a new boulevard that was to serve the new civic campus, and the construction of the Henley Street Bridge; but the Plan's most ambitious project, and most of its esthetic beautification recommendations, were ignored and soon forgotten.

Over the next 60 years, little park land was added to the city. Billboard restrictions remained loose. The riverfront, that "great asset," was eventually paved over. Residents fled the city for the suburbs in even greater numbers than they had when planners worried about the cost of suburbanization. And 16 years after the Plan was proposed and rejected, author John Gunther visited, working on what would be an international bestseller called Inside U.S.A. In it, he called 1945 Knoxville "the ugliest city…in America."

Post-Utopia

If there's a lesson here, it's not to ignore Utopians. We may forget that some wild plans have actually succeeded, at least in some form. If the World's Fair hadn't gotten off the ground in the early '80s, it would be included in this survey. The Great Smoky Mountains National Park—a place where ordinary people could get away from the smoky cities and hike and camp under the stars and breathe fresh air—must have seemed like a pipe dream to some when it was first discussed before World War I. The federal government clearly wasn't ready for such a huge purchase, and the mountaineers and the lumber industry wouldn't think of giving up that much land without a fight. Knoxville's well-heeled dreamers had their way with that fantasy.

And there's the Tennessee Valley Authority. In its early years, TVA was arguably the most utopian scheme ever hatched by the federal government: hardly less than an attempt to rebuild civilization from scratch, and maybe get it right this time. Knoxville became its brain center, mainly because of the city's proximity to the planned dam-building town of Norris, which was to be the crucible of a new socioeconomic ideal. Arthur Morgan, TVA's first chairman, saw his chief role as engineer of this model community, overlord of this New Deal Shangri-La, where everyone would live in esthetic harmony. To show his faith, Morgan moved there.

Morgan was fired, and over the years his utopian ideals dwindled. But even after 65 years, TVA remains a very unusual utility company in that it has a major "nonpower" component. Nonpower TVA has had a significant influence on the life of Knoxville for more than six decades.

It almost goes without saying, when you're talking about human beings: The reality always falls short of the ideal. But often, the post-ideal reality is at least better than the pre-ideal reality was.

If it has lost its hotel and college, Fountain City still has its heart-shaped pond and is a more pleasant place to visit than it would have been without the fundamentalist utopians of a century ago. Leftover Talahi monuments make Sequoyah Hills a more interesting neighborhood than most upscale suburbs are. Throw in Arthur Morgan's Norris and it's clear that several of the area's most distinctive residential communities are places that were meant to be much more than they are.

Volunteer Landing and the riverfront Holston and Lakeshore parks might be recognizable to the City Planning Commission of 1929 as partial realizations of their ideals. The Metropolitan Planning Commission itself, spiritual descendant of Louis Brownlow's City Planning Commission, still comes up with provocative proposals about what might still be possible in this city.

Unrealistic, high-minded, and doomed though they may be, Utopians throw unknown variables into our daily routine, leave us perplexed and restless and sometimes inspired. And they often leave interesting rubble for our kids to climb on.

To be thorough, each column should have its own bibliography. The bulk of the stories in these columns came from Knoxville newspapers, most of which are available on microfilm through the Knox County library system (all the way back to 1791), and from biographies and other histories which are also mostly in the public library.

The following regional histories are essential sources I have found repeatedly helpful.

Encyclopedia of East Tennessee, Jim Stokely and Jeff D. Johnson, editors. Children's Museum of Oak Ridge, 1981.

The French Broad - Holston Country, Mary Utopia Rothrock, editor. East Tennessee Historical Society, 1946.

Heart of the Valley: A History of Knoxville, Tennessee, Lucille Deaderick, editor. East Tennessee Historical Society, 1976. (This volume includes Dr. William J. MacArthur's excellent capsule essay, "Knoxville's History: An Interpretation.")

Humphrey, Steve, *That D——d Brownlow*, Appalachian Consortium Press, 1978.

McDonald, Michael J. and William Bruce Wheeler, *Knoxville, Tennessee: Continuity And Change In an Appalachian City.* University of Tennessee Press, 1983.

Montgomery, James Riley, Stanley J. Folmsbee, and Lee Seifert Greene, *To Foster Knowledge: A History of the University of Tennessee, 1794-1970,* University of Tennessee Press, 1984.

Seymour, Digby, *Divided Loyalties,* University of Tennessee Press, 1963; rev. East Tennessee Historical Society, 1982.

Wolfe, Charles K., *Tennessee Strings: the Story of Country Music in Tennessee*, University of Tennessee Press, 1977.

I'd also like to thank the Lawson McGhee Library and its annex, the McClung Collection, where I found more than half of the information I've used in these stories; the University of Tennessee Library and McClung Museum's archives; and the East Tennessee Historical Society.

In addition, I'd like to thank each of the following individuals, who have been particularly helpful in researching more than one column, either personally or through their research filed in the library: Ron Allen, Stephen V. Ash, Paul Ashdown, David Babelay, Ted Behr, Jeff Bills, Bob Booker, Steve Cotham, Allison Ensor, David Harkness, Nelda Hill, Robert McGinnis, Andrew Nelson, Andrea Ray, Donna Young, and everybody around the big mahogany bar at the Great Southern Brewing Company.

JACK NEELY